6. Enter your class ID code to join a class.

IF YOU HAVE A CLASS CODE FROM YOUR TEACHER

a. Enter your class code and click [Next]

b. Once you have joined a class, you will be able to use the Discussion Board and Email tools.

c. To enter this code later, choose **Join a Class**.

IF YOU DO NOT HAVE A CLASS CODE

a. If you do not have a class ID code, click [Skip]

b. You do not need a class ID code to use *iQ Online*.

c. To enter this code later, choose **Join a Class**.

7. Review registration information and click Log In. Then choose your book. Click **Activities** to begin using *iQ Online*.

IMPORTANT

- After you register, the next time you want to use *iQ Online*, go to www.iQOnlinePractice.com and log in with your email address and password.
- The online content can be used for 12 months from the date you register.
- For help, please contact customer service: eltsupport@oup.com.

WHAT IS iQ ONLINE ?

All new activities provide essential skills **practice** and support.

Vocabulary and Grammar **games** immerse you in the language and provide even more practice.

Authentic, engaging **videos** generate new ideas and opinions on the Unit Question.

Go to the Media Center to download or stream all **student book audio**.

Use the **Discussion Board** to discuss the Unit Question and more.

Email encourages communication with your teacher and classmates.

Automatic grading gives immediate feedback and tracks progress.

Progress Reports show what you have mastered and where you still need more practice.

OXFORD
UNIVERSITY PRESS

198 Madison Avenue
New York, NY 10016 USA

Great Clarendon Street, Oxford, OX2 6DP, United Kingdom

Oxford University Press is a department of the University of Oxford.
It furthers the University's objective of excellence in research, scholarship,
and education by publishing worldwide. Oxford is a registered trade
mark of Oxford University Press in the UK and in certain other countries

Director, ELT New York: Laura Pearson
Head of Adult, ELT New York: Stephanie Karras
Publisher: Sharon Sargent
Managing Editor: Mariel DeKranis
Development Editor: Eric Zuarino
Head of Digital, Design, and Production: Bridget O'Lavin
Executive Art and Design Manager: Maj-Britt Hagsted
Design Project Manager: Debbie Lofaso
Content Production Manager: Julie Armstrong
Senior Production Artist: Elissa Santos
Image Manager: Trisha Masterson
Image Editor: Liaht Ziskind
Production Coordinator: Brad Tucker

ISBN: 978 0 19 481840 7 Student Book 1 with iQ Online pack
ISBN: 978 0 19 481841 4 Student Book 1 as pack component
ISBN: 978 0 19 481802 5 iQ Online student website

Printed in China
This book is printed on paper from certified and well-managed sources.

ACKNOWLEDGEMENTS

Illustrations by: 4 Barb Bastian; p. 22 Barb Bastian; p. 28 Barb Bastian; p. 56
5W Infographics; p. 76 Bill Smith Group; p. 100 Barb Bastian; p. 103 Jean
Tuttle; p. 144 Greg Paprocki; p. 158 Barb Bastian; p. 168 Barb Bastian; p. 182
Jean Tuttle.

*We would also like to thank the following for permission to reproduce the following
photographs*: Cover: David Pu'u/Corbis; Inside back cover: lvcandy/Getty
Images, Bloom Design/shutterstock; Video Vocabulary (used throughout
the book): Oleksiy Mark / Shutterstock; p. 2/3 JONATHAN ALCORN/Corbis
UK Ltd.; p. 4 Blend Images/Alamy (office); p. 4 Image Source/Getty Images
(waiter); p. 4 Juice Images/Getty Images (store); p. 4 Steve Hix/Somos
Images/Corbis UK Ltd. (teacher); p. 6 Blend Images/Alamy; p. 18 PhotoAlto/
Oxford University Press; p. 26 Yaacov Dagan/Alamy; p. 26/27 George H.H.
Huey/Alamy; p. 27 laurentiu iordache/Alamy (masks); p. 27 Gianni Dagli
Orti/Corbis UK Ltd. (aztec); p. 36 Manfred Rutz/Getty Images (greeting);
p. 36 Chad Ehlers/Alamy (reading); p. 36 Stock Connection Distribution/
Alamy (flowers); p. 36 amana images inc./Alamy (card); p. 40 Photodisc/
Oxford University Press; p. 45 Julie Armstrong/Oxford University Press
(sphinx); p. 45 Julie Armstrong/Oxford University Press (flowers); p. 45 Julie
Armstrong/Oxford University Press (Rocks); p. 50 Kameleon007 /iStockphoto
(instruments); p. 50 epa european pressphoto agency b.v./Alamy (balloons);
p. 51 eye35 stock/Alamy (keyring); p. 51 Africa Studio/Shutterstock

(suitcase); p. 52 Nataliya Popova/Shutterstock (no littering); p. 52 RATOCA/
Shutterstock (camera); p. 52 Arcady/Shutterstock (flowers); p. 52 ValeStock/
Shutterstock (bird); p. 52 Evgenia Bolyukh/Shutterstock (fire); p. 52 Zanna
Art/Shutterstock (grass); p. 55 Anna Yu/Alamy (bus); p. 55 Larry Lilac/Oxford
University Press (wall); p. 55 imageBROKER/Alamy (boat); p. 55 Frans Lanting
Studio/Alamy (penguins); p. 59 Jon Arnold Images Ltd/Alamy (eiffel); p. 59
Philipus/Alamy (buji); p. 59 Lonely Planet Images/Alamy (waterfall); p. 59
Imagebroker/Alamy (mountains); p. 61 Paul Springett 08/Alamy (Machu
Picchu); p. 61 Kiselev Andrey Valerevich/Shutterstock (backpacker); p. 61
Bob Daemmrich/Alamy (teacher); p. 61 Adrian Sherratt/Alamy (painting);
p. 61 Milla Kontkanen/Alamy (beach); p. 65 Sarmu/Getty Images; p. 67
John Harper/Corbis UK Ltd.; p. 74/75 Tom Merton/Getty Images; p. 76
Mango Productions/Corbis UK Ltd.; p. 78 AF archive/Alamy (Dickens); p. 78
Classic Image/Alamy (house); p. 78 19th era/Alamy (dinner); p. 81 Oxford
University Press; p. 85 Photodisc/Oxford University Press; p. 98 ANDREW
YATES / Stringer/Getty Images; p. 99 herreid /iStockphoto (badminton);
p. 99 tarasov/Shutterstock (sports gear); p. 100 Christophe Simon/AFP/Getty
Images (swimmer); p. 100 Hemera/Thinkstock (baseball); p. 100 Polka Dot
Images/Oxford University Press (cyclist); p. 100 Aspen Photo/Shutterstock
(basketball); p. 104 James Oliver/Oxford University Press (track); p. 104
Photodisc/Oxford University Press (race); p. 107 Photodisc/Oxford University
Press (tennis); p. 107 Image Source/Oxford University Press (training);
p. 107 Jim West/Alamy (hockey); p. 107 Photodisc/Oxford University Press
(karate); p. 107 Photodisc/Oxford University Press (cycling); p. 120/121
Spencer Grant / Art Directors/Alamy; p. 122 Nycretoucher/Getty Images;
p. 125 www.jupiterimages.com/Getty Images; p. 127 DreamPictures/Getty
Images (woman); p. 127 Mint Images - Tim Robbins/Getty Images (man);
p. 128 RubberBall/Alamy; p. 130 CandyBox Images/Shutterstock; p. 134
Erik Isakson/Getty Images; p. 142/143 Rana Faure/Corbis UK Ltd.; p. 146
Photodisc/Oxford University Press; p. 150 PhotoAlto/Laurence Mouton/
Oxford University Press; p. 162 Matt Hess/Golden Pixels Llc/Corbis UK Ltd.;
p. 166 Stephen Frink/Getty Images; p. 166/167 wacpan/Shutterstock; p. 167
2011 Gamma-Rapho/Getty Images (rollercoaster); p. 167 UNIVERSAL / THE
KOBAL COLLECTION/Kobal Collection (birds); p. 168 James Gerholdt/Peter
Arnold Images/Getty Images (snake); p. 168 PhotoAlto/Alamy (elevator);
p. 168 PhotosIndia.com/Getty Images (speaker); p. 168 Alex Benwell/Alamy
(skyscrapers); p. 168 Barry Mason/Alamy (airplane); p. 168 LorenRyePhoto/
Alamy (lightning); p. 172 William Radcliffe/Science Faction/Corbis UK Ltd.;
p. 174 David Wall/Alamy; p. 176 James W. Porter/Corbis UK Ltd.; p. 177
Kiichiro Sato/AP Photo/Press Association Images; p. 178 Pegaz/Alamy; p. 185
Don Johnston/Getty Images; Back Cover: mozcann/iStockphoto.

SHAPING learning TOGETHER

We would like to acknowledge the teachers from all over the world who participated in the development process and review of the Q series.

Special thanks to our *Q: Skills for Success* Second Edition Topic Advisory Board

Shaker Ali Al-Mohammad, Buraimi University College, Oman; **Dr. Asmaa A. Ebrahim**, University of Sharjah, U.A.E.; **Rachel Batchilder**, College of the North Atlantic, Qatar; **Anil Bayir**, Izmir University, Turkey; **Flora Mcvay Bozkurt**, Maltepe University, Turkey; **Paul Bradley**, University of the Thai Chamber of Commerce Bangkok, Thailand; **Joan Birrell-Bertrand**, University of Manitoba, MB, Canada; **Karen E. Caldwell**, Zayed University, U.A.E.; **Nicole Hammond Carrasquel**, University of Central Florida, FL, U.S.; **Kevin Countryman**, Seneca College of Applied Arts & Technology, ON, Canada; **Julie Crocker**, Arcadia University, NS, Canada; **Marc L. Cummings**, Jefferson Community and Technical College, KY, U.S.; **Rachel DeSanto**, Hillsborough Community College Dale Mabry Campus, FL, U.S.; **Nilüfer Ertürkmen**, Ege University, Turkey; **Sue Fine**, Ras Al Khaimah Women's College (HCT), U.A.E.; **Amina Al Hashami**, Nizwa College of Applied Sciences, Oman; **Stephan Johnson**, Nagoya Shoka Daigaku, Japan; **Sean Kim**, Avalon, South Korea; **Gregory King**, Chubu Daigaku, Japan; **Seran Küçük**, Maltepe University, Turkey; **Jonee De Leon**, VUS, Vietnam; **Carol Lowther**, Palomar College, CA, U.S.; **Erin Harris-MacLeod**, St. Mary's University, NS, Canada; **Angela Nagy**, Maltepe University, Turkey; **Huynh Thi Ai Nguyen**, Vietnam; **Daniel L. Paller**, Kinjo Gakuin University, Japan; **Jangyo Parsons**, Kookmin University, South Korea; **Laila Al Qadhi**, Kuwait University, Kuwait; **Josh Rosenberger**, English Language Institute University of Montana, MT, U.S.; **Nancy Schoenfeld**, Kuwait University, Kuwait; **Jenay Seymour**, Hongik University, South Korea; **Moon-young Son**, South Korea; **Matthew Taylor**, Kinjo Gakuin Daigaku, Japan; **Burcu Tezcan-Unal**, Zayed University, U.A.E.; **Troy Tucker**, Edison State College-Lee Campus, FL, U.S.; **Kris Vicca**, Feng Chia University, Taichung; **Jisook Woo**, Incheon University, South Korea; **Dunya Yenidunya**, Ege University, Turkey

UNITED STATES **Marcarena Aguilar**, North Harris College, TX; **Rebecca Andrade**, California State University North Ridge, CA; **Lesley Andrews**, Boston University, MA; **Deborah Anholt**, Lewis and Clark College, OR; **Robert Anzelde**, Oakton Community College, IL; **Arlys Arnold**, University of Minnesota, MN; **Marcia Arthur**, Renton Technical College, WA; **Renee Ashmeade**, Passaic County Community College, NJ; **Anne Bachmann**, Clackamas Community College, OR; **Lida Baker**, UCLA, CA; **Ron Balsamo**, Santa Rosa Junior College, CA; **Lori Barkley**, Portland State University, OR; **Eileen Barlow**, SUNY Albany, NY; **Sue Bartch**, Cuyahoga Community College, OH; **Lora Bates**, Oakton High School, VA; **Barbara Batra**, Nassau County Community College, NY; **Nancy Baum**, University of Texas at Arlington, TX; **Rebecca Beck**, Irvine Valley College, CA; **Linda Berendsen**, Oakton Community College, IL; **Jennifer Binckes Lee**, Howard Community College, MD; **Grace Bishop**, Houston Community College, TX; **Jean W. Bodman**, Union County College, NJ; **Virginia Bouchard**, George Mason University, VA; **Kimberley Briesch Sumner**, University of Southern California, CA; **Kevin Brown**, University of California, Irvine, CA; **Laura Brown**, Glendale Community College, CA; **Britta Burton**, Mission College, CA; **Allison L. Callahan**, Harold Washington College, IL; **Gabriela Cambiasso**, Harold Washington College, IL; **Jackie Campbell**, Capistrano Unified School District, CA; **Adele C. Camus**, George Mason University, VA; **Laura Chason**, Savannah College, GA; **Kerry Linder Catana**, Language Studies International, NY; **An Cheng**, Oklahoma State University, OK; **Carole Collins**, North Hampton Community College, PA; **Betty R. Compton**, Intercultural Communications College, HI; **Pamela Couch**, Boston University, MA; **Fernanda Crowe**, Intrax International Institute, CA; **Vicki Curtis**, Santa Cruz, CA; **Margo Czinski**, Washtenaw Community College, MI; **David Dahnke**, Lone Star College, TX; **Gillian M. Dale**, CA; **L. Dalgish**, Concordia College, MN; **Christopher Davis**, John Jay College, NY; **Sherry Davis**, Irvine University, CA; **Natalia de Cuba**, Nassau County Community College, NY; **Sonia Delgadillo**, Sierra College, CA; **Esmeralda Diriye**, Cypress College & Cal Poly, CA; **Marta O. Dmytrenko-Ahrabian**, Wayne State University, MI; **Javier Dominguez**, Central High School, SC; **Jo Ellen Downey-Greer**, Lansing Community College, MI; **Jennifer Duclos**, Boston University, MA; **Yvonne Duncan**, City College of San Francisco, CA; **Paul Dydman**, USC Language Academy, CA; **Anna Eddy**, University of Michigan-Flint, MI; **Zohan El-Gamal**, Glendale Community College, CA; **Jennie Farnell**, University of Connecticut, CT; **Susan Fedors**, Howard Community College, MD; **Valerie Fiechter**, Mission College, CA; **Ashley Fifer**, Nassau County Community College, NY; **Matthew Florence**, Intrax International Institute, CA; **Kathleen Flynn**, Glendale College, CA; **Elizabeth Fonsea**, Nassau County Community College, NY; **Eve Fonseca**, St. Louis Community College, MO; **Elizabeth Foss**, Washtenaw Community College, MI; **Duff C. Galda**, Pima Community College, AZ; **Christiane Galvani**, Houston Community College, TX; **Gretchen Gerber**, Howard Community College, MD; **Ray Gonzalez**, Montgomery College, MD; **Janet Goodwin**, University of California, Los Angeles, CA; **Alyona Gorokhova**, Grossmont College, CA; **John Graney**, Santa Fe College, FL; **Kathleen Green**, Central High School, AZ; **Nancy Hamadou**, Pima Community College-West Campus, AZ; **Webb Hamilton**, De Anza College, San Jose City College, CA; **Janet Harclerode**, Santa Monica Community College, CA; **Sandra Hartmann**, Language and Culture Center, TX; **Kathy Haven**, Mission College, CA; **Roberta Hendrick**, Cuyahoga Community College, OH; **Ginny Heringer**, Pasadena City College, CA; **Adam Henricksen**, University of Maryland, MD; **Carolyn Ho**, Lone Star College-CyFair, TX; **Peter Hoffman**, LaGuardia Community College, NY; **Linda Holden**, College of Lake County, IL; **Jana Holt**, Lake Washington Technical College, WA; **Antonio Iccarino**, Boston University, MA; **Gail Ibele**, University of Wisconsin, WI; **Nina Ito**, American Language Institute, CSU Long Beach, CA; **Linda Jensen**, UCLA, CA; **Lisa Jurkowitz**, Pima Community College, CA; **Mandy Kama**, Georgetown University, Washington, DC; **Stephanie Kasuboski**, Cuyahoga Community College, OH; **Chigusa Katoku**, Mission College, CA; **Sandra Kawamura**, Sacramento City College, CA; **Gail Kellersberger**, University of Houston-Downtown, TX; **Jane Kelly**, Durham Technical Community College, NC; **Maryanne Kildare**, Nassau County Community College, NY; **Julie Park Kim**, George Mason University, VA; **Kindra Kinyon**, Los Angeles Trade-Technical College, CA; **Matt Kline**, El Camino College, CA; **Lisa Kovacs-Morgan**, University of California, San Diego, CA; **Claudia Kupiec**, DePaul University, IL; **Renee La Rue**, Lone Star College-Montgomery, TX; **Janet Langon**, Glendale College, CA; **Lawrence Lawson**, Palomar College, CA; **Rachele Lawton**, The Community College of Baltimore County, MD; **Alice Lee**, Richland College, TX; **Esther S. Lee**, CSUF & Mt. SAC, CA; **Cherie Lenz-Hackett**, University of Washington, WA; **Joy Leventhal**, Cuyahoga Community College, OH; **Alice Lin**, UCI Extension, CA; **Monica Lopez**, Cerritos College, CA; **Dustin Lovell**, FLS International Marymount College, CA; **Carol Lowther**, Palomar College, CA; **Candace Lynch-Thompson**, North Orange County Community College District, CA; **Thi Thi Ma**, City College of San Francisco, CA; **Steve Mac Isaac**, USC Long Academy, CA; **Denise Maduli-Williams**, City College of San Francisco, CA; **Eileen Mahoney**, Camelback High School, AZ; **Naomi Mardock**, MCC-Omaha, NE; **Brigitte Maronde**, Harold Washington College, IL; **Marilyn Marquis**, Laposita College CA; **Doris Martin**, Glendale Community College; Pasadena City College, CA; **Keith Maurice**, University of Texas at Arlington, TX; **Nancy Mayer**, University of Missouri-St. Louis, MO; **Aziah McNamara**, Kansas State University, KS; **Billie McQuillan**, Education Heights, MN; **Karen Merritt**, Glendale Union High School District, AZ; **Holly Milkowart**, Johnson County Community College, KS; **Eric Moyer**, Intrax International Institute, CA; **Gino Muzzatti**, Santa Rosa Junior College, CA; **Sandra Navarro**, Glendale Community College, CA; **Than Nyeinkhin**, ELAC, PCC, CA; **William Nedrow**, Triton College, IL; **Eric Nelson**, University of Minnesota, MN; **Than Nyeinkhin**, ELAC, PCC, CA; **Fernanda Ortiz**, Center for English as a Second Language at the University of Arizona, AZ; **Rhony Ory**, Ygnacio Valley High School, CA; **Paul Parent**, Montgomery College, MD; **Dr. Sumeeta Patnaik**, Marshall University, WV; **Oscar Pedroso**, Miami Dade College, FL; **Robin Persiani**, Sierra College, CA; **Patricia Prenz-Belkin**, Hostos Community College, NY; **Suzanne Powell**, University of Louisville, KY; **Jim Ranalli**, Iowa State University, IA; **Toni R. Randall**, Santa Monica College, CA; **Vidya Rangachari**, Mission College, CA; **Elizabeth Rasmussen**, Northern Virginia Community College, VA; **Lara Ravitch**, Truman College, IL;

Deborah Repasz, San Jacinto College, TX; Marisa Recinos, English Language Center, Brigham Young University, UT; Andrey Reznikov, Black Hills State University, SD; Alison Rice, Hunter College, NY; Jennifer Robles, Ventura Unified School District, CA; Priscilla Rocha, Clark County School District, NV; Dzidra Rodins, DePaul University, IL; Maria Rodriguez, Central High School, AZ; Josh Rosenberger, English Language Institute University of Montana, MT; Alice Rosso, Bucks County Community College, PA; Rita Rozzi, Xavier University, OH; Maria Ruiz, Victor Valley College, CA; Kimberly Russell, Clark College, WA; Stacy Sabraw, Michigan State University, MI; Irene Sakk, Northwestern University, IL; Deborah Sandstrom, University of Illinois at Chicago, IL; Jenni Santamaria, ABC Adult, CA; Shaeley Santiago, Ames High School, IA; Peg Sarosy, San Francisco State University, CA; Alice Savage, North Harris College, TX; Donna Schaeffer, University of Washington, WA; Karen Marsh Schaeffer, University of Utah, UT; Carol Schinger, Northern Virginia Community College, VA; Robert Scott, Kansas State University, KS; Suell Scott, Sheridan Technical Center, FL; Shira Seaman, Global English Academy, NY; Richard Seltzer, Glendale Community College, CA; Harlan Sexton, CUNY Queensborough Community College, NY; Kathy Sherak, San Francisco State University, CA; German Silva, Miami Dade College, FL; Ray Smith, Maryland English Institute, University of Maryland, MD; Shira Smith, NICE Program University of Hawaii, HI; Tara Smith, Felician College, NJ; Monica Snow, California State University, Fullerton, CA; Elaine Soffer, Nassau County Community College, NY; Andrea Spector, Santa Monica Community College, CA; Jacqueline Sport, LBWCC Luverne Center, AL; Karen Stanely, Central Piedmont Community College, NC; Susan Stern, Irvine Valley College, CA; Ayse Stromsdorfer, Soldan I.S.H.S., MO; Yilin Sun, South Seattle Community College, WA; Thomas Swietlik, Intrax International Institute, IL; Nicholas Taggert, University of Dayton, OH; Judith Tanka, UCLA Extension–American Language Center, CA; Amy Taylor, The University of Alabama Tuscaloosa, AL; Andrea Taylor, San Francisco State, CA; Priscilla Taylor, University of Southern California, CA; Ilene Teixeira, Fairfax County Public Schools, VA; Shirl H. Terrell, Collin College, TX; Marya Teutsch-Dwyer, St. Cloud State University, MN; Stephen Thergesen, ELS Language Centers, CO; Christine Tierney, Houston Community College, TX; Arlene Turini, North Moore High School, NC; Cara Tuzzolino, Nassau County Community College, NY; Suzanne Van Der Valk, Iowa State University, IA; Nathan D. Vasarhely, Ygnacio Valley High School, CA; Naomi S. Verratti, Howard Community College, MD; Hollyahna Vettori, Santa Rosa Junior College, CA; Julie Vorholt, Lewis & Clark College, OR; Danielle Wagner, FLS International Marymount College, CA; Lynn Walker, Coastline College, CA; Laura Walsh, City College of San Francisco, CA; Andrew J. Watson, The English Bakery; Donald Weasenforth, Collin College, TX; Juliane Widner, Sheepshead Bay High School, NY; Lynne Wilkins, Mills College, CA; Pamela Williams, Ventura College, CA; Jeff Wilson, Irvine Valley College, CA; James Wilson, Consumnes River College, CA; Katie Windahl, Cuyahoga Community College, OH; Dolores "Lorrie" Winter, California State University at Fullerton, CA; Jody Yamamoto, Kapi'olani Community College, HI; Ellen L. Yaniv, Boston University, MA; Norman Yoshida, Lewis & Clark College, OR; Joanna Zadra, American River College, CA; Florence Zysman, Santiago Canyon College, CA;

CANADA Patricia Birch, Brandon University, MB; Jolanta Caputa, College of New Caledonia, BC; Katherine Coburn, UBC's ELI, BC; Erin Harris-Macleod, St. Mary's University, NS; Tami Moffatt, English Language Institute, BC; Jim Papple, Brock University, ON; Robin Peace, Confederation College, BC;

ASIA Rabiatu Abubakar, Eton Language Centre, Malaysia; Wiwik Andreani, Bina Nusantara University, Indonesia; Frank Bailey, Baiko Gakuin University, Japan; Mike Baker, Kosei Junior High School, Japan; Leonard Barrow, Kanto Junior College, Japan; Herman Bartelen, Japan; Siren Betty, Fooyin University, Kaohsiung; Thomas E. Bieri, Nagoya College, Japan; Natalie Brezden, Global English House, Japan; MK Brooks, Mukogawa Women's University, Japan; Truong Ngoc Buu, The Youth Language School, Vietnam; Charles Cabell, Toyo University, Japan; Fred Carruth, Matsumoto University, Japan; Frances Causer, Seijo University, Japan; Jeffrey Chalk, SNU, South Korea; Deborah Chang, Wenzao Ursuline College of Languages, Kaohsiung; David Chatham, Ritsumeikan University, Japan; Andrew Chih Hong Chen, National Sun Yat-sen University, Kaohsiung; Christina Chen, Yu-Tsai Bilingual Elementary School, Taipei; Hui-chen Chen, Shi-Lin High School of Commerce, Taipei; Seungmoon Choe, K2M Language Institute, South Korea; Jason Jeffree Cole, Coto College, Japan; Le Minh Cong, Vungtau Tourism Vocational College, Vietnam; Todd Cooper, Toyama National College of Technology, Japan; Marie Cosgrove, Daito Bunka

University, Japan; Randall Cotten, Gifu City Women's College, Japan; Tony Cripps, Ritsumeikan University, Japan; Andy Cubalit, CHS, Thailand; Daniel Cussen, Takushoku University, Japan; Le Dan, Ho Chi Minh City Electric Power College, Vietnam; Simon Daykin, Banghwa-dong Community Centre, South Korea; Aimee Denham, ILA, Vietnam; Bryan Dickson, David's English Center, Taipei; Nathan Ducker, Japan University, Japan; Ian Duncan, Simul International Corporate Training, Japan; Nguyen Thi Kieu Dung, Thang Long University, Vietnam; Truong Quang Dung, Tien Giang University, Vietnam; Nguyen Thi Thuy Duong, Vietnamese American Vocational Training College, Vietnam; Wong Tuck Ee, Raja Tun Azlan Science Secondary School, Malaysia; Emilia Effendy, International Islamic University Malaysia, Malaysia; Bettizza Escueta, KMUTT, Thailand; Robert Eva, Kaisei Girls High School, Japan; Jim George, Luna International Language School, Japan; Jurgen Germeys, Silk Road Language Center, South Korea; Wong Ai Gnoh, SMJK Chung Hwa Confucian, Malaysia; Sarah Go, Seoul Women's University, South Korea; Peter Goosselink, Hokkai High School, Japan; Robert Gorden, SNU, South Korea; Wendy M. Gough, St. Mary College/Nunoike Gaigo Senmon Gakko, Japan; Tim Grose, Sapporo Gakuin University, Japan; Pham Thu Ha, Le Van Tam Primary School, Vietnam; Ann-Marie Hadzima, Taipei; Troy Hammond, Tokyo Gakugei University International Secondary School, Japan; Robiatul 'Adawiah Binti Hamzah, SMK Putrajaya Precinct 8(1), Malaysia; Tran Thi Thuy Hang, Ho Chi Minh City Banking University, Vietnam; To Thi Hong Hanh, CEFALT, Vietnam; George Hays, Tokyo Kokusai Daigaku, Japan; Janis Hearn, Hongik University, South Korea; Chantel Hemmi, Jochi Daigaku, Japan; David Hindman, Sejong University, South Korea; Nahn Cam Hoa, Ho Chi Minh City University of Technology, Vietnam; Jana Holt, Korea University, South Korea; Jason Hollowell, Nihon University, Japan; F. N. (Zoe) Hsu, National Tainan University, Yong Kang; Kuei-ping Hsu, National Tsing Hua University, Hsinchu City; Wenhua Hsu, I-Shou University, Kaohsiung; Luu Nguyen Quoc Hung, Cantho University, Vietnam; Cecile Hwang, Changwon National University, South Korea; Ainol Haryati Ibrahim, Universiti Malaysia Pahang, Malaysia; Robert Jeens, Yonsei University, South Korea; Linda M. Joyce, Kyushu Sangyo University, Japan; Dr. Nisai Kaewsanchai, English Square Kanchanaburi, Thailand; Aniza Kamarulzaman, Sabah Science Secondary School, Malaysia; Ikuko Kashiwabara, Osaka Electro-Communication University, Japan; Gurmit Kaur, INTI College, Malaysia; Nick Keane, Japan; Ward Ketcheson, Aomori University, Japan; Nicholas Kemp, Kyushu International University, Japan; Montchatry Ketmuni, Rajamangala University of Technology, Thailand; Dinh Viet Khanh, Vietnam; Seonok Kim, Kangsu Jongro Language School, South Korea; Suyeon Kim, Anyang University, South Korea; Kelly P. Kimura, Soka University, Japan; Masakazu Kimura, Katoh Gakuen Gyoshu High School, Japan; Gregory King, Chubu Daigaku, Japan; Stan Kirk, Konan University, Japan; Donald Knight, Nan Hua/Fu Li Junior High Schools, Hsinchu; Kari J. Kostiainen, Nagoya City University, Japan; Pattri Kuanpulpol, Silpakorn University, Thailand; Ha Thi Lan, Thai Binh Teacher Training College, Vietnam; Eric Edwin Larson, Miyazaki Prefectural Nursing University, Japan; David Laurence, Chubu Daigaku, Japan; Richard S. Lavin, Prefectural University of Kumamoto, Japan; Shirley Leane, Chugoku Junior College, Japan; I-Hsiu Lee, Yunlin; Nari Lee, Park Jung PLS, South Korea; Tae Lee, Yonsei University, South Korea; Lys Yongsoon Lee, Reading Town Geumcheon, South Korea; Mallory Leece, Sun Moon University, South Korea; Dang Hong Lien, Tan Lam Upper Secondary School, Vietnam; Huang Li-Han, Rebecca Education Institute, Taipei; Sovannarith Lim, Royal University of Phnom Penh, Cambodia; Ginger Lin, National Kaohsiung Hospitality College, Kaohsiung; Noel Lineker, New Zealand/Japan; Tran Dang Khanh Linh, Nha Trang Teachers' Training College, Vietnam; Daphne Liu, Buliton English School, Taipei; S. F. Josephine Liu, Tien-Mu Elementary School, Taipei; Caroline Luo, Tunghai University, Taichung; Jeng-Jia Luo, Tunghai University, Taichung; Laura MacGregor, Gakushuin University, Japan; Amir Madani, Visuttharangsi School, Thailand; Elena Maeda, Sacred Heart Professional Training College, Japan; Vu Thi Thanh Mai, Hoang Gia Education Center, Vietnam; Kimura Masakazu, Kato Gakuen Gyoshu High School, Japan; Susumu Matsuhashi, Net Link English School, Japan; James McCrostie, Daito Bunka University, Japan; Joel McKee, Inha University, South Korea; Colin McKenzie, Wachirawit Primary School, Thailand; Terumi Miyazoe, Tokyo Denki Daigaku, Japan; William K. Moore, Hiroshima Kokusai Gakuin University, Japan; Kevin Mueller, Tokyo Kokusai Daigaku, Japan; Hudson Murrell, Baiko Gakuin University, Japan; Frances Namba, Senri International School of Kwansei Gakuin, Japan; Keiichi Narita, Niigata University, Japan; Kim Chung Nguyen, Ho Chi Minh University of

Industry, Vietnam; **Do Thi Thanh Nhan**, Hanoi University, Vietnam; **Dale Kazuo Nishi**, Aoyama English Conversation School, Japan; **Huynh Thi Ai Nguyen**, Vietnam; **Dongshin Oh**, YBM PLS, South Korea; **Keiko Okada**, Dokkyo Daigaku, Japan; **Louise Ohashi**, Shukutoku University, Japan; **Yongjun Park**, Sangji University, South Korea; **Donald Patnaude**, Ajarn Donald's English Language Services, Thailand; **Virginia Peng**, Ritsumeikan University, Japan; **Suangkanok Piboonthamnont**, Rajamangala University of Technology, Thailand; **Simon Pitcher**, Business English Teaching Services, Japan; **John C. Probert**, New Education Worldwide, Thailand; **Do Thi Hoa Quyen**, Ton Duc Thang University, Vietnam; **John P. Racine**, Dokkyo University, Japan; **Kevin Ramsden**, Kyoto University of Foreign Studies, Japan; **Luis Rappaport**, Cung Thieu Nha Ha Noi, Vietnam; **Lisa Reshad**, Konan Daigaku Hyogo, Japan; **Peter Riley**, Taisho University, Japan; **Thomas N. Robb**, Kyoto Sangyo University, Japan; **Rory Rosszell**, Meiji Daigaku, Japan; **Maria Feti Rosyani**, Universitas Kristen Indonesia, Indonesia; **Greg Rouault**, Konan University, Japan; **Chris Ruddenklau**, Kindai University, Japan; **Hans-Gustav Schwartz**, Thailand; **Mary-Jane Scott**, Soongsil University, South Korea; **Dara Sheahan**, Seoul National University, South Korea; **James Sherlock**, A.P.W. Angthong, Thailand; **Prof. Shieh**, Minghsin University of Science & Technology, Xinfeng; **Yuko Shimizu**, Ritsumeikan University, Japan; **Suzila Mohd Shukor**, Universiti Sains Malaysia, Malaysia; **Stephen E. Smith**, Mahidol University, Thailand; **Moon-young Son**, South Korea; **Seunghee Son**, Anyang University, South Korea; **Mi-young Song**, Kyungwon University, South Korea; **Lisa Sood**, VUS, BIS, Vietnam; **Jason Stewart**, Taejon International Language School, South Korea; **Brian A. Stokes**, Korea University, South Korea; **Mulder Su**, Shih-Chien University, Kaohsiung; **Yoomi Suh**, English Plus, South Korea; **Yun-Fang Sun**, Wenzao Ursuline College of Languages, Kaohsiung; **Richard Swingle**, Kansai Gaidai University, Japan; **Sanford Taborn**, Kinjo Gakuin Daigaku, Japan; **Mamoru Takahashi**, Akita Prefectural University, Japan; **Tran Hoang Tan**, School of International Training, Vietnam; **Takako Tanaka**, Doshisha University, Japan; **Jeffrey Taschner**, American University Alumni Language Center, Thailand; **Matthew Taylor**, Kinjo Gakuin Daigaku, Japan; **Michael Taylor**, International Pioneers School, Thailand; **Kampanart Thammaphati**, Wattana Wittaya Academy, Thailand; **Tran Duong The**, Sao Mai Language Center, Vietnam; **Tran Dinh Tho**, Duc Tri Secondary School, Vietnam; **Huynh Thi Anh Thu**, Nhatrang College of Culture Arts and Tourism, Vietnam; **Peter Timmins**, Peter's English School, Japan; **Fumie Togano**, Hosei Daini High School, Japan; **F. Sigmund Topor**, Keio University Language School, Japan; **Tu Trieu**, Rise VN, Vietnam; **Yen-Cheng Tseng**, Chang-Jung Christian University, Tainan; **Pei-Hsuan Tu**, National Cheng Kung University, Tainan City; **Hajime Uematsu**, Hirosaki University, Japan; **Rachel Um**, Mok-dong Oedae English School, South Korea; **David Underhill**, EEExpress, Japan; **Ben Underwood**, Kugenuma High School, Japan; **Siriluck Usaha**, Sripatum University, Thailand; **Tyas Budi Utami**, Indonesia; **Nguyen Thi Van**, Far East International School, Vietnam; **Stephan Van Eycken**, Kosei Gakuen Girls High School, Japan; **Zisa Velasquez**, Taihu International School/Semarang International School, China/Indonesia; **Jeffery Walter**, Sangji University, South Korea; **Bill White**, Kinki University, Japan; **Yohanes De Deo Widyastoko**, Xaverius Senior High School, Indonesia; **Dylan Williams**, SNU, South Korea; **Jisuk Woo**, Ichean University, South Korea; **Greg Chung-Hsien Wu**, Providence University, Taichung; **Xun Xiaoming**, BLCU, China; **Hui-Lien Yeh**, Chai Nan University of Pharmacy and Science, Tainan; **Sittiporn Yodnil**, Huachiew Chalermprakiet University, Thailand; **Shamshul Helmy Zambahari**, Universiti Teknologi Malaysia, Malaysia; **Ming-Yuli**, Chang Jung Christian University, Tainan; **Aimin Fadhlee bin Mahmud Zuhodi**, Kuala Terengganu Science School, Malaysia;

TURKEY **Shirley F. Akis**, American Culture Association/Fomara; **Gül Akkoç**, Boğaziçi University; **Seval Akmeşe**, Haliç University; **Ayşenur Akyol**, Ege University; **Ayşe Umut Aribaş**, Beykent University; **Gökhan Asan**, Kapadokya Vocational College; **Hakan Asan**, Kapadokya Vocational College; **Julia Asan**, Kapadokya Vocational College; **Azarvan Atac**, Piri Reis University; **Nur Babat**, Kapadokya Vocational College; **Feyza Balakbabalar**, Kadir Has University; **Gözde Balikçi**, Beykent University; **Deniz Balım**, Haliç University; **Asli Başdoğan**, Kadir Has University; **Ayla Bayram**, Kapadokya Vocational College; **Pinar Bilgiç**, Kadir Has University; **Kenan Bozkurt**, Kapadokya Vocational College; **Yonca Bozkurt**, Ege University; **Frank Carr**, Piri Reis; **Mengü Noyan Çengel**, Ege University; **Elif Doğan**, Ege University; **Natalia Donmez**, 29 Mayis Üniversite; **Nalan Emirsoy**, Kadir Has University; **Ayşe Engin**, Kadir Has University; **Ayhan Gedikbaş**, Ege University; **Gülşah Gençer**, Beykent University; **Seyit Ömer Gök**, Gediz University; **Tuğba Gök**, Gediz University; **İlkay Gökçe**, Ege University; **Zeynep Birinci Guler**, Maltepe University; **Neslihan Güler**, Kadir Has University; **Sircan Gümüş**, Kadir Has University; **Nesrin Gündoğu**, T.C. Piri Reis University; **Tanju Gurpinar**, Piri Reis University; **Selin Gurturk**, Piri Reis University; **Neslihan Gurutku**, Piri Reis University; **Roger Hewitt**, Maltepe University; **Nilüfer İbrahimoğlu**, Beykent University; **Nevin Kaftelen**, Kadir Has University; **Sultan Kalin**, Kapadokya Vocational College; **Sema Kaplan Karabina**, Anadolu University; **Eray Kara**, Giresun University; **Beylü Karayazgan**, Ege University; **Darren Kelso**, Piri Reis University; **Trudy Kittle**, Kapadokya Vocational College; **Şaziye Konaç**, Kadir Has University; **Güneş Korkmaz**, Kapadokya Vocational College; **Robert Ledbury**, Izmir University of Economics; **Ashley Lucas**, Maltepe University; **Bülent Nedium Uça**, Dogus University; **Murat Nurlu**, Ege University; **Mollie Owens**, Kadir Has University; **Oya Özağaç**, Boğaziçi University; **Funda Özcan**, Ege University; **İlkay Özdemir**, Ege University; **Ülkü Öztürk**, Gediz University; **Cassondra Puls**, Anadolu University; **Yelda Sarikaya**, Cappadocia Vocational College; **Müge Şekercioğlu**, Ege University; **Melis Senol**, Canakkale Onsekiz Mart University, The School of Foreign Languages; **Patricia Sümer**, Kadir Has University; **Rex Surface**, Beykent University; **Mustafa Torun**, Kapadokya Vocational College; **Tansel Üstünloğlu**, Ege University; **Fatih Yücel**, Beykent University; **Şule Yüksel**, Ege University;

THE MIDDLE EAST **Amina Saif Mohammed Al Hashamia**, Nizwa College of Applied Sciences, Oman; **Jennifer Baran**, Kuwait University, Kuwait; **Phillip Chappells**, GEMS Modern Academy, U.A.E.; **Sharon Ruth Devaneson**, Ibri College of Technology, Oman; **Hanaa El-Deeb**, Canadian International College, Egypt; **Yvonne Eaton**, Community College of Qatar, Qatar; **Brian Gay**, Sultan Qaboos University, Oman; **Gail Al Hafidh**, Sharjah Women's College (HCT), U.A.E.; **Jonathan Hastings**, American Language Center, Jordan; **Laurie Susan Hilu**, English Language Centre, University of Bahrain, Bahrain; **Abraham Irannezhad**, Mehre Aval, Iran; **Kevin Kempe**, CNA-Q, Qatar; **Jill Newby James**, University of Nizwa; **Mary Kay Klein**, American University of Sharjah, U.A.E.; **Sian Khoury**, Fujairah Women's College (HCT), U.A.E.; **Hussein Dehghan Manshadi**, Farhang Pajooh & Jaam-e-Jam Language School, Iran; **Jessica March**, American University of Sharjah, U.A.E.; **Neil McBeath**, Sultan Qaboos University, Oman; **Sandy McDonagh**, Abu Dhabi Men's College (HCT), U.A.E.; **Rob Miles**, Sharjah Women's College (HCT), U.A.E.; **Michael Kevin Neumann**, Al Ain Men's College (HCT), U.A.E.;

LATIN AMERICA **Aldana Aguirre**, Argentina; **Claudia Almeida**, Coordenação de Idiomas, Brazil; **Cláudia Arias**, Brazil; **Maria de los Angeles Barba**, FES Acatlan UNAM, Mexico; **Lilia Barrios**, Universidad Autónoma de Tamaulipas, Mexico; **Adán Beristain**, UAEM, Mexico; **Ricardo Böck**, Manoel Ribas, Brazil; **Edson Braga**, CNA, Brazil; **Marli Buttelli**, Mater et Magistra, Brazil; **Alessandra Campos**, Inova Centro de Linguas, Brazil; **Priscila Catta Preta Ribeiro**, Brazil; **Gustavo Cestari**, Access International School, Brazil; **Walter D'Alessandro**, Virginia Language Center, Brazil; **Lilian De Gennaro**, Argentina; **Mônica De Stefani**, Quality Centro de Idiomas, Brazil; **Julio Alejandro Flores**, BUAP, Mexico; **Mirian Freire**, CNA Vila Guilherme, Brazil; **Francisco Garcia**, Colegio Lestonnac de San Angel, Mexico; **Miriam Giovanardi**, Brazil; **Darlene Gonzalez Miy**, ITESM CCV, Mexico; **Maria Laura Grimaldi**, Argentina; **Luz Dary Guzmán**, IMPAHU, Colombia; **Carmen Koppe**, Brazil; **Monica Krutzler**, Brazil; **Marcus Murilo Lacerda**, Seven Idiomas, Brazil; **Nancy Lake**, CEL-LEP, Brazil; **Cris Lazzerini**, Brazil; **Sandra Luna**, Argentina; **Ricardo Luvisan**, Brazil; **Jorge Murilo Menezes**, ACBEU, Brazil; **Monica Navarro**, Instituto Cultural A. C., Mexico; **Joacyr Oliveira**, Faculdades Metropolitanas Unidas and Summit School for Teachers, Brazil; **Ayrton Cesar Oliveira de Araujo**, E&A English Classes, Brazil; **Ana Laura Oriente**, Seven Idiomas, Brazil; **Adelia Peña Clavel**, CELE UNAM, Mexico; **Beatriz Pereira**, Summit School, Brazil; **Miguel Perez**, Instituto Cultural, Mexico; **Cristiane Perone**, Associação Cultura Inglesa, Brazil; **Pamela Claudia Pogré**, Colegio Integral Caballito / Universidad de Flores, Argentina; **Dalva Prates**, Brazil; **Marianne Rampaso**, Iowa Idiomas, Brazil; **Daniela Rutolo**, Instituto Superior Cultural Británico, Argentina; **Maione Sampaio**, Maione Carrijo Consultoria em Inglês Ltda, Brazil; **Elaine Santesso**, TS Escola de Idiomas, Brazil; **Camila Francisco Santos**, UNS Idiomas, Brazil; **Lucia Silva**, Cooplem Idiomas, Brazil; **Maria Adela Sorzio**, Instituto Superior Santa Cecilia, Argentina; **Elcio Souza**, Unibero, Brazil; **Willie Thomas**, Rainbow Idiomas, Brazil; **Sandra Villegas**, Instituto Humberto de Paolis, Argentina; **John Whelan**, La Universidad Nacional Autonoma de Mexico, Mexico

v

CONTENTS

UNIT **1**

Business

NOTE TAKING ▶	writing key words and main ideas
LISTENING ▶	listening for key words and phrases
VOCABULARY ▶	distinguishing between words with similar meanings
GRAMMAR ▶	simple present and simple past
PRONUNCIATION ▶	simple past -ed
SPEAKING ▶	asking for repetition and clarification

Q

UNIT QUESTION

How can you find a good job?

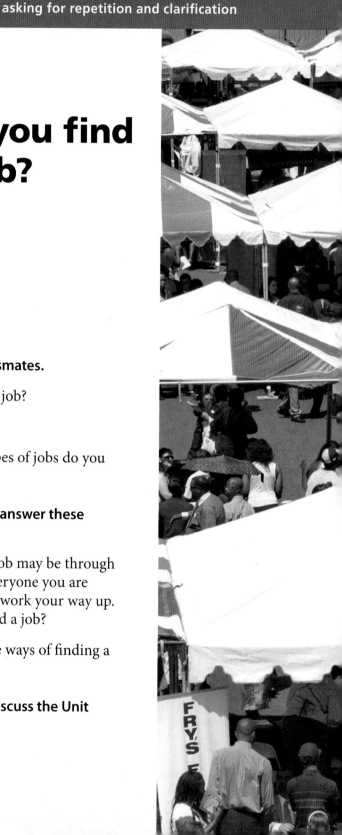

A Discuss these questions with your classmates.

1. Do you have a job? What is your dream job?

2. How do people find jobs?

3. Look at the photo of a job fair. What types of jobs do you see? Why are the people at this job fair?

B Listen to *The Q Classroom* online. Then answer these questions.

1. Marcus says that the best way to find a job may be through friends. Sophy thinks you should tell everyone you are looking for work. Felix says you have to work your way up. What do you think is the best way to find a job?

2. What experience do you have with these ways of finding a job? Other ways?

iQ ONLINE **C** Go to the Online Discussion Board to discuss the Unit Question with your classmates.

UNIT
OBJECTIVE ▶▶▶▶ Listen to a conversation and two interviews. Gather information and ideas to role-play a job interview.

3

D Match the ads with the jobs in the photos. More than one answer is possible.

1. *tempor incididunt ut labore et dolore*
   Must have excellent computer skills

2. *labore et dolore*
   Need a college education
   Email résumé to:

3. *do eiusmod tempor incididunt*
   Need three years of experience

4. *skills. One to two years of experience years of*
   Must enjoy working with people
   Must be organized. Need excellent computer

web designer ____

salesperson ____

server ____

teacher ____

E Tell a partner which job you like best, and why.

> **A:** *I like the web designer job. I have excellent computer skills.*
>
> **B:** *Really? I prefer the salesperson position. I like working with people.*

When you take notes, you write only a few words and phrases about the most important points. If you try to write too much, you will miss important information. Learn to listen for the main ideas and write the key words and phrases that will help you remember them. Make two columns on your paper and label them *Key Words* and *Main Ideas* as in the example below. As you listen, write the key words in the left column. After you listen, use the key words to fill in additional information about the main ideas in the right column.

Read this transcript from a TV news report about important job skills for university students.

> Many college students today do not have the basic skills needed to succeed in a full-time job after they graduate. According to a recent study, universities need to do more to prepare students for the workplace.

Look at the note page below. Notice the key words and main ideas.

Key Words	Main Ideas
Students don't have skills – full-time job	College students don't have skills to succeed in a full-time job after they graduate.
Study: universities need to prepare students	Study: Universities need to do more to prepare students for work.

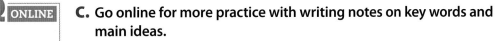

A. Listen to the next part of the news report. Make two columns for key words and main ideas. Take notes on the key words.

B. Use the key words you wrote to write the main ideas. Compare notes with a partner.

C. Go online for more practice with writing notes on key words and main ideas.

LISTENING

LISTENING 1 | Looking for a Job

UNIT OBJECTIVE ▶▶▶▶ You are going to listen to two students discuss summer jobs. They find a website with a video called "Careers at Braxton Books." As you listen to the conversation, gather information and ideas about how you can find a good job.

PREVIEW THE LISTENING

A. **VOCABULARY** Here are some words from Listening 1. Read the sentences. Then write each <u>underlined</u> word next to the correct definition.

1. Khalid wants to change his <u>career</u>. He wants to become a doctor.

2. Haya starts her new job tomorrow. She's a new <u>employee</u> of that company.

3. A college education is one <u>requirement</u> to be a teacher. You also need some teaching experience.

4. I don't know much about computers. I can only do <u>basic</u> things, like type papers and use email.

5. Our server isn't very <u>organized</u>. He forgot to bring your coffee, and he brought me the wrong food.

6. Education is important. It's harder to get some jobs if you don't have a college <u>degree</u>.

7. I want to get a job at Rick's Café. I just have to complete this <u>application</u> and take it to the restaurant.

8. I have an <u>interview</u> next week at a computer company.

a. _____ (*noun*) a person who works for someone

b. _____ (*noun*) a paper you get when you finish college

c. _____ (*noun*) a job that you learn to do and then do for many years

d. _____ (*noun*) a special piece of paper you fill out when you try to get a job

e. _____ (*noun*) something that you need or that you must do or have

f. _____ (*adjective*) able to plan your work or life well

Oxford 2000 keywords

g. _____ (*noun*) a meeting when someone asks you
   questions to decide if you will get a job

h. _____ (*adjective*) simple; including only what is necessary

B. Go online for more practice with the vocabulary.

C. **PREVIEW** Two students are looking online for a summer job.
They find a website with a video called "Careers at Braxton Books."

Check (✓) the topics you think the video will include.

☐ how to buy books online   ☐ how to get an application

☐ job requirements   ☐ store hours

WORK WITH THE LISTENING

A. **LISTEN AND TAKE NOTES** Listen to the conversation. Take notes on
the key words. Follow the sample notes on page 5.

B. Listen to the conversation again. Add notes about the main ideas
based on the key words you wrote.

C. Read the statements. Write *T* (true) or *F* (false). Then correct any false
statements. Write the words or phrases from your notes that helped
you get the answer.

_F_ 1. Ben works at Braxton Books now.

   Ben doesn't work at Braxton Books yet. _____

   Words and phrases: wants to work there this summer _____

___ 2. Braxton Books is a big company.

   _____

   Words and phrases: _____

___ 3. The company sells books in stores and online.

   _____

   Words and phrases: _____

___ 4. The company has some open jobs.

   _____

   Words and phrases: _____

_____ 5. Ben will probably try to get a job at Braxton Books.

_____

Words and phrases: _____

D. Circle the answer that best completes each statement.

1. Braxton Books plans to ____ .
   a. open a new store   b. continue its success   c. start an e-book business

2. Salespeople at Braxton Books have to ____ .
   a. work only online   b. have a college degree   c. help a lot of customers

3. Most Web designers at Braxton Books are ____ .
   a. highly trained   b. college students   c. friendly people

4. The company only accepts applications ____ .
   a. on its website   b. in person   c. after an interview

E. Match the sentence halves to form true statements.

_____ 1. Ben is looking for   a. a salesperson position.

_____ 2. Braxton Books is   b. a summer job.

_____ 3. You need basic computer skills for   c. to work on a team.

_____ 4. Web designers need   d. an international company.

_____ 5. A new part of Braxton's business is   e. a lot of experience.

_____ 6. Salespeople must like   f. an e-book business.

Tip for Success

Speakers sometimes use certain phrases to signal a list of important information. Some examples are *here are,* *the following are,* and *here is a list of.*

F. Listen to the excerpt from Listening 1. Complete the job requirements for each job in the chart.

Salesperson	Web designer
• _____ years' experience	• _____ years' experience
• basic _____	• _____ skills
• organized	• _____ in Web design
• friendly	(preferred)
• enjoy _____	• organized
_____	• have _____ ideas

SAY WHAT YOU THINK

Discuss the questions in a group.

Critical Thinking **Tip**

Question 1 asks you to **compare** the two jobs. **Comparing** means you notice the things that are the same for both jobs. Comparing can help you remember important points about the two things.

1. Look again at the chart in Activity F on page 8. What requirements are necessary for both jobs at Braxton Books?

2. Do you meet the requirements for the jobs? Which ones?

3. Which student in your group is the best person for each job at Braxton Books?

Listening Skill	Listening for key words and phrases

Key words and **phrases** tell you the important information about a topic. Speakers often repeat key words and phrases more than once. Listening for key words and phrases can help you identify the topic of a conversation.

 Listen to the example from Listening 1.

The topic of the conversation is *looking for a summer job.*

The key words and phrases are *work there this summer, job,* and *careers.* The speakers say the words *summer* and *jobs* more than once.

A. Ben and Saud are listening to the information video for Braxton Books. Listen for key words and phrases in each section. Circle the main topic.

1. a. careers at Braxton Books
   b. the company's history and success
   c. the number of employees

2. a. jobs at Braxton Books
   b. how to get an application
   c. job interviews

3. a. store hours
   b. computer skills
   c. job requirements

4. a. job interviews
   b. how to get an application
   c. how to buy online books

B. Listen again. Check (✓) the words and phrases the speaker uses more than once.

1. ☐ interest in careers   3. ☐ requirements
   ☐ growing   ☐ college degree
   ☐ over 200 stores   ☐ years of experience
   ☐ success   ☐ interesting

2. ☐ job   4. ☐ interested
   ☐ positions   ☐ one of our stores
   ☐ great people   ☐ application
   ☐ join our team   ☐ interview

iQ ONLINE | **C.** Go online for more practice with listening for key words and phrases.

LISTENING 2 | The Right Person for the Job

UNIT OBJECTIVE ▶▶▶ You are going to listen to the manager of an advertising company. He is interviewing two people for a Web designer position. As you listen to the interviews, gather information and ideas about how you can find a good job.

PREVIEW THE LISTENING

A. **VOCABULARY** Here are some words from Listening 2. Read their definitions. Then complete each sentence below with the correct word.

> **advertising** (*noun*) telling people about things to buy
> **assistant** (*noun*) a person who helps someone in a more important position
> **graduate** (*verb*) to finish your studies at a school, college, or university
> **major** (*noun*) the main subject you study in college
> **manager** (*noun*) 🔑 the person who controls a company or business
> **résumé** (*noun*) a list of your education and work experience that you send when you are trying to get a job

🔑 Oxford 2000 keyword

1. My mother speaks French very well. French was her _____ in college.

2. Juan got a job as a(n) _____ in a school. He'll help the children when the teacher is busy.

3. It isn't easy to get a job in _____. You need to have interesting ideas, and you have to know how to sell things.

4. I sent my _____ to ten companies. Only one company called me for an interview.

5. My father is the _____ of a large restaurant. He has a lot of employees, and he's very busy.

6. I plan to _____ from college next year.

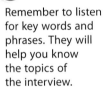 **B.** Go online for more practice with the vocabulary.

C. **PREVIEW** You are going to listen to Mark Williamson, the manager of New World Design Advertising Company. He is going to interview Tom and George for a Web designer position.

 for Success

Remember to listen for key words and phrases. They will help you know the topics of the interview.

Check (✓) the interview questions you think Mark will ask.

☐ Can you tell me a little about yourself?
☐ What was your major in college?
☐ How old are you?
☐ Do you have any experience in advertising?
☐ What are your best qualities?
☐ Are you married?
☐ Do you have any questions?

WORK WITH THE LISTENING

A. **LISTEN AND TAKE NOTES** In the first interview, Mark interviews Tom. Listen and take notes on the key words. See the sample below.

Mark	Tom
Tell me about yourself.	Came to NY from Chicago

B. In the second interview, Mark interviews George. Listen and take notes on the key words.

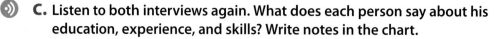

C. Listen to both interviews again. What does each person say about his education, experience, and skills? Write notes in the chart.

	Education	Experience	Skills
1. Tom			
2. George			

D. Read the sentences. Circle the word or phrase that best completes each sentence.

1. The company is in (New York / Chicago / London).

2. Tom has a lot of (design experience / computer skills / questions).

3. In college, Tom worked at a (company / restaurant / store).

4. Mark does not ask Tom about his (résumé / personality / experience).

5. George says he was very (busy / organized / friendly) in college.

6. George has a good (job / personality / idea) for the position.

E. Complete each sentence with a word from the box. You will use some words more than once.

education   experience   skills

1. Tom talks mostly about his _____ .

2. Tom has a lot of useful _____ for Web design.

3. Tom does not have the _____ necessary for the job.

4. George has _____ as an office assistant in an advertising agency.

5. George's _____ does not relate to advertising.

F. Read the sentences. Then check (✓) *True, Probably true, Probably not true,* or *Not true.*

	True	Probably true	Probably not true	Not true
1. Tom graduated from college.	☐	☐	☐	☐
2. Tom wishes he had more experience.	☐	☐	☐	☐
3. Mark will choose Tom for the job.	☐	☐	☐	☐
4. George's college major was design.	☐	☐	☐	☐
5. George enjoys working with people.	☐	☐	☐	☐
6. George is the right person for the job.	☐	☐	☐	☐

G. Go online to listen to *What Makes a Good Manager?* and check your comprehension.

SAY WHAT YOU THINK

A. Discuss the questions in a group.

1. Which person should get the job in Listening 2? Why?

   A: I think . . . should get the job. . . . He has . . .
   B: I disagree. I think . . .

2. Have you ever been on a job interview? What other questions can people ask?

B. Before you watch the video, discuss the questions in a group.

1. What special skills do you need for the job you want?

2. How can people learn new job skills?

C. Go online to watch the video about learning new skills to get a job. Then check your comprehension.

VIDEO VOCABULARY

make a living *(phr. v.)* earn money to buy the things you need in life

pathway *(n.)* a way to achieve something

training *(v.)* making yourself ready for something by studying or doing something a lot

D. Think about the unit video, Listening 1, and Listening 2 as you discuss the questions.

1. What steps do people take to find a job?

2. With your group, think of three interesting jobs. What are the best ways to find out about job openings and the best ways to train for each job?

Vocabulary Skill | Distinguishing between words with similar meanings

Some words have **similar meanings**, but they are used in different situations. The definitions and example sentences in the dictionary can help you decide which word is best to use.

Look at the dictionary entries and example sentences for *career* and *work*.

ca·reer 🔑 /kəˈrɪr/ *noun* [*count*] a job that you learn to do and then do for many years: *He is considering a **career in** teaching.* ◆ *His career was always more important to him than his family.* ➲ Look at the note at **job**.	**work²** 🔑 /wərk/ *noun* **1** [*noncount*] the job that you do to earn money: *I'm looking for work* ◆ *What time do you **start** work?* ◆ *How long have you been **out of work** (= without a job)?* ➲ Look at the note at **job**.

> Max graduated from college last year. He's ready to start a **career**.
> I have to leave for **work** very early tomorrow morning.

The definition of *career*, as you can see, is a job you want or plan to do for a long time. *Work* is a more general word meaning the job you do for money.

Always look for both words in the dictionary before deciding which one to use.

All dictionary entries are from the *Oxford Basic American Dictionary for learners of English* © Oxford University Press 2011.

A. Read the dictionary entries. Circle the best word for each sentence.

job 🔑 **AWL** /dʒɑb/ *noun* [*count*] **1** the work that you do for money: *She **got a job** as a waitress.* ◆ *Peter just **lost** his job.*	**ca·reer** 🔑 /kəˈrɪr/ *noun* [*count*] a job that you learn to do and then do for many years: *He is considering a **career in** teaching.* ◆ *His career was always more important to him than his family.* ➲ Look at the note at **job**.

1. A (job / career) in law can be very demanding.

2. My company closed. I need to find another (job / career) soon.

com·pa·ny 🔑 /ˈkʌmpəni/ *noun (plural* com·pa·nies*)*
1 [*count*] (**BUSINESS**) a group of people who work together to make or sell things: *an advertising company* • *the Student Loans Company* ⮕ The short way of writing "Company" in names is Co.: *Milton and Co.*
2 [*noncount*] being with a person or people: *I always enjoy Mark's company.*

busi·ness 🔑 /ˈbɪznəs/ *noun (plural* busi·ness·es*)*
1 [*noncount*] buying and selling things: *I want to go into business when I leave school.* • *Business is not very good this year.*
2 [*noncount*] the work that you do as your job: *The manager will be away on business next week.* • *a business trip*

3. Jim went into (company / business) with his brother.

4. The (company / business) has over 6,000 employees around the world.

B. Write one new sentence for each word in Activity A.

1. (job) _____

_____

2. (career) _____

_____

3. (company) _____

_____

4. (business) _____

_____

C. Go online for more practice with distinguishing between words with similar meanings.

SPEAKING

At the end of this unit, you are going to role-play a job interview with a partner using the interview questions on page 23. As you speak, you will need to ask for repetition and clarification.

Grammar   *Part 1* Simple present

- Use the simple present to talk about facts or general truths.
  Braxton Books **is** a big company.   I **enjoy** working with people.

Simple present statements with regular verbs

Affirmative	Negative
I / You **like** working on a team.	I / You **do not like** this job.
He / She / It **wants** to change careers.	He / She / It **does not want** to be a manager.
We / You / They **sell** computers.	We / You / They **do not sell** advertising.

- Use the simple present to describe habits and routines.
  We **take** the train to the office.   I **do not work** on Fridays.

Simple present statements with *be*

Affirmative	Negative
I **am** friendly.	I **am not** a server.
You **are** organized.	You **are not** organized.
He / She / It **is** on time.	He / She / It **is not** on time.
We / You / They **are** college students.	We / You / They **are not** employees.

- Use the simple present to describe states and feelings.
  You **are** very friendly.   I **want** a career as a Web designer.

Simple present statements with *have*

Affirmative	Negative
I / You **have** a college degree.	I / You **do not have** a résumé.
He / She / It **has** a few questions.	He / She / It **does not have** the application.
We / You / They **have** 600 employees.	We / You / They **do not have** an office in New York.

A. Circle the correct verb to complete each sentence.

1. A Web designer (need / needs) a lot of experience, but I only (have / has) one year.

2. It (is not / does not) easy to find a job these days, especially if you (want / wants) a good career.

3. I (have / has) a college degree, and I (am / is) a hard worker.

4. The company does not (accept / accepts) applications online. They (prefer / prefers) to meet you in person.

5. The manager (like / likes) your résumé, but we (do not / does not) have any open positions.

6. She (are not / is not) very organized, but she (enjoy / enjoys) working on a team.

Grammar   *Part 2* Simple past

Use the **simple past** to talk about actions that happened in the past.

Regular verbs
- To form the simple past, add **-ed** to the base form of the verb.

  I work**ed** at a clothing store last summer. I help**ed** customers.

- For verbs ending in *e*, add **-d**.

  I serve**d** dinner at a busy restaurant. I also prepare**d** takeout orders.

- For verbs ending in *y*, drop the *y* and add **-ied**.

  Tom app**lied** for a position as a Web designer. He stud**ied** Web design in college.

Irregular verbs

The verb *be* is irregular in the simple past. It has two forms: *was* and *were*.

  My internship **was** a good experience. The people I worked with **were** great.

Here are some other verbs with irregular simple past forms.

say	**said**	have	**had**	come	**came**
make	**made**	know	**knew**	see	**saw**
go	**went**	take	**took**	get	**got**
do	**did**				

> **Negative statements**
> - To form a negative statement, use *didn't* + the base form of the verb.
>
> I **didn't graduate** from high school last year. It was two years ago.

A. Complete each sentence with the simple past form of the verb.

Mark: Well, let's get started. Please sit down, Tom. . . . OK. Can you tell me

a little about yourself?

Tom: Sure. I _____ to New York a few months ago from
1. (come)

Chicago. I _____ to Chicago School of Design.
2. (go)

Mark: Yes, I _____ that on your résumé. Yes, here it is. You
3. (see)

_____ last May. What did you study there?
4. (graduate)

Tom: I'm sorry. I didn't catch that. Could you say that again, please?

Mark: Sure. What _____ your major in college?
5. (be)

Tom: Well, I _____ my degree in design. I _____
6. (get)   7. (take)

a lot of computer classes, too. I _____ to use my design
8. (want)

and computer skills. That's why I want a career in Web design.

B. Practice the conversation in Activity A with a partner.

C. Read the notes an interviewer wrote about Carlos. Then read the interview questions below. Write your own answers to the questions.

> 1. from Caracas, Venezuela; graduated from Central University in 2009
>
> 2. major was computer science, studied English
>
> 3. was a Web designer for one year; before that, was a waiter

1. Can you tell me a little about yourself?

2. What did you study in high school/college?

3. What work experience do you have?

D. Take turns asking and answering the job interview questions in Activity C with your partner. Use your notes.

E. Go online for more practice with the simple present and the simple past.

F. Go online for the grammar expansion.

Pronunciation | **Simple past -ed**

The simple past of a regular verb ends in *-ed*. The pronunciation of this final sound depends on the sound at the end of the base verb. There are three possible sounds.

- The *-ed* = /d/ when the sound is **voiced** (with sound). This includes all vowel sounds, and the consonants /b/, /g/, /dʒ/ (ju**dg**ed), /l/, /m/, /n/, /r/, /v/, and /z/.

- The *-ed* = /t/ when the sound is **unvoiced** (without sound), including /f/, /k/, /p/, /s/, /ʃ/ (wi**sh**), and /tʃ/ (wa**tch**).

- The *-ed* = /əd/ when the final sound is either the voiced sound /d/ or the unvoiced sound /t/.

Read and listen to the examples in the chart.

If the verb ends in . . .	Base verb	Simple past
• a voiced sound, pronounce the past with /d/.	enjoy	enjoy**ed**
	study	stud**ied**
	learn	learn**ed**
• an unvoiced sound, pronounce the past with /t/.	laugh	laugh**ed**
	work	work**ed**
	help	help**ed**
	wash	wash**ed**
• a /t/ or /d/, pronounce the past with /əd/.	graduate	graduat**ed**
	end	end**ed**

A. Work with a partner. Take turns saying the simple past forms of the verbs in the box.

change	like	need	require	study	walk
complete	look	prefer	stop	wait	want

B. Write the simple past form of each verb in Activity A in the correct column. Then listen and check your answers.

/t/	/d/	/əd/
	changed	

C. Read the conversations and <u>underline</u> the regular verbs in the simple past. Write /d/, /t/, or /əd/ above each verb ending to tell its correct pronunciation.

1. **A:** I <u>completed</u>/əd/ an application for a job at Jim's Pizza today.

   B: Oh, I worked at Jim's Pizza last summer. I washed dishes there. It was fun.

   A: Really? That's good. I wanted to work at Paul's Café, but they said I needed more experience.

   B: Yeah, they chose someone else for the job.

   A: Who?

   B: Me.

2. **A:** Please sit down, Mr. Smith. Did you bring your application?

   B: I completed it online, and I emailed it. Is that OK?

   A: Oh, yes. Here it is. I printed it this morning. . . . Now, can you tell me a little about yourself?

   B: Yes, I graduated from Franklin High School in 2010. I wanted to get some work experience before college. So, I joined a computer training program.

   A: I see. Did you finish the program?

   B: Yes, I finished it last week.

D. Practice the conversations in Activity C with your partner. Check your partner's pronunciation of the simple past.

iQ ONLINE **E.** Go online for more practice with pronouncing the simple past with *-ed*.

When you listen, sometimes you need to ask the speaker to repeat information. Here are some phrases you can use when you don't hear or understand something well.

I'm sorry. I didn't catch that. Could you say that again, please?

Could you repeat that? Do you mean . . . ?

A. Listen to the excerpt from Listening 2. Check (✓) the phrases Tom uses.

☐ I didn't catch that. ☐ Could you say that again, please?

☐ Could you repeat that? ☐ Do you mean . . . ?

B. Listen and complete each conversation with a phrase for repetition and clarification.

1. **Miteb:** Hello?

   Fahad: Hello, is this Miteb?

   Miteb: Yes, it is.

   Fahad: Oh, hi, Miteb. It's Fahad from All-Tech Computers. Thank you for coming to the interview this morning. I forgot to ask you about . . .

   Miteb: Hello? _____.

2. **Interviewer:** Great. OK, thanks. And can you tell me a little about your experience in Australia? I saw on your résumé that . . .

   Liam: _____?

3. **Waleed:** Hey, Jamal! How are you doing?

   Jamal: Oh, hi, Waleed. I'm great! I just found out that . . .

   Waleed: Sorry, Jamal. _____?

4. **Andrew:** What do you plan to do after you graduate, Seth?

   Seth: Well, I had a meeting with the manager of New World Designs last week.

   Andrew: A meeting? _____?

C. Take turns reading the conversations in Activity B with a partner.

D. Go online for more practice with asking for repetition and clarification.

Tip for Success

It may be impolite in some cultures, but it's important to ask for clarification in English-speaking countries when you don't understand something. Begin with *I'm sorry* or *excuse me* to be more polite.

**UNIT
OBJECTIVE** ▶▶▶▶

In this assignment, you are going to role-play a job interview with a partner. As you prepare your role-play, think about the Unit Question, "How can you find a good job?" Use information from Listening 1, Listening 2, the unit video, and your work in the unit to support your role-play. Refer to the Self-Assessment checklist on page 24.

CONSIDER THE IDEAS

A. Work with a partner. Match each job with the correct advertisement.

____ 1. office assistant

____ 2. tour guide

____ 3. video game tester

____ 4. children's sports coach

____ 5. house painter

____ 6. high school English teacher

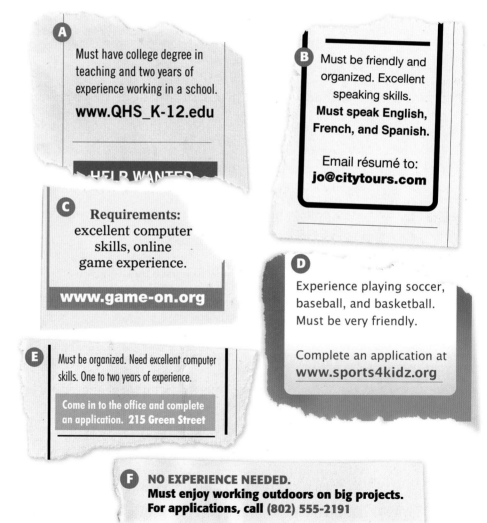

A Must have college degree in teaching and two years of experience working in a school.
www.QHS_K-12.edu

HELP WANTED

B Must be friendly and organized. Excellent speaking skills. **Must speak English, French, and Spanish.**

Email résumé to:
jo@citytours.com

C Requirements: excellent computer skills, online game experience.
www.game-on.org

D Experience playing soccer, baseball, and basketball. Must be very friendly.

Complete an application at
www.sports4kidz.org

E Must be organized. Need excellent computer skills. One to two years of experience.
Come in to the office and complete an application. **215 Green Street**

F **NO EXPERIENCE NEEDED.**
Must enjoy working outdoors on big projects.
For applications, call (802) 555-2191

B. Read the ads again. <u>Underline</u> the job requirements for each ad.

C. Work in a group. Which jobs in Activity A do you want to have? Do you meet the requirements? Tell your group.

"I want to be an office assistant. I'm organized and have good computer skills."

PREPARE AND SPEAK

A. GATHER IDEAS Work with a partner. Think of a job you want to have. Together, list the requirements for that job and your partner's job.

B. ORGANIZE IDEAS Imagine you are going to an interview for your job from Activity A. The interviewer asks you these questions. How do you answer?

1. Can you tell me a little about yourself? _____

    _____

2. What did you study in high school or college? _____

    _____

3. What work experience do you have? _____

    _____

4. What skills do you have? _____

    _____

5. Do you have any questions? _____

    _____

C. SPEAK Role-play the interview with your partner. Use the interview questions from Activity B. Take notes on your partner's answers. Refer to the Self-Assessment checklist on page 24 before you begin.

A: Hello, I'm _____. Please have a seat.

B: Thank you. It's nice to meet you, _____.

A: OK. Let's get started.

    (Question 1) _____

B: (Answer) _____

A: (Question 2) _____

B: (Answer) _____

A: (Question 3) _____

B: (Answer) _____

A: (Question 4) _____

B: (Answer) _____

A: (Question 5) _____

B: (Answer) _____

iQ ONLINE **Go online for your alternate Unit Assignment.**

CHECK AND REFLECT

A. CHECK Think about the Unit Assignment as you complete the Self-Assessment checklist.

SELF-ASSESSMENT		
Yes	No	
☐	☐	I was able to speak easily about the topic.
☐	☐	I took notes on key words and main ideas.
☐	☐	My partner/group/class understood me.
☐	☐	I used statements in the simple present and the simple past.
☐	☐	I used vocabulary from the unit.
☐	☐	I asked for repetition and clarification.
☐	☐	I pronounced the simple past of regular verbs correctly.

iQ ONLINE **B. REFLECT** Go to the Online Discussion Board to discuss these questions.

1. What is something new you learned in this unit?

2. Think about the Unit Question—How can you find a good job? Is your answer different now than when you started the unit? If yes, how is it different? Why?

TRACK YOUR SUCCESS

Circle the words and phrases you have learned in this unit.

Nouns
advertising
application
assistant AWL
business 🔑
career 🔑
company 🔑
degree 🔑
employee
interview 🔑
job 🔑
major AWL
manager 🔑
requirement AWL
résumé
work 🔑

Verb
graduate

Adjectives
basic 🔑
organized 🔑

Phrases
Could you repeat that?
Could you say that
  again, please?
Do you mean . . . ?
I'm sorry. I didn't
  catch that.

🔑 Oxford 2000 keywords
AWL Academic Word List

Check (✓) the skills you learned. If you need more work on a skill, refer to the page(s) in parentheses.

NOTE TAKING ■	I can take notes on key words and main ideas. (p. 5)
LISTENING ■	I can listen for key words and phrases. (p. 9)
VOCABULARY ■	I can use the dictionary to distinguish between words with similar meanings. (p. 14)
GRAMMAR ■	I can recognize and use the simple present and the simple past. (pp. 16 and 17)
PRONUNCIATION ■	I can pronounce simple past -ed endings. (p. 19)
SPEAKING ■	I can ask for repetition and clarification. (p. 21)
UNIT OBJECTIVE ▶▶▶ ■	I can gather information and ideas to role-play a job interview.

NOTE TAKING	▶	taking notes in a T-chart
LISTENING	▶	listening for main ideas and details
VOCABULARY	▶	words in context
GRAMMAR	▶	*should/shouldn't; it's* + adjective + infinitive
PRONUNCIATION	▶	the schwa /ə/ sound
SPEAKING	▶	presenting information from notes

UNIT QUESTION

Why do we study other cultures?

A Discuss these questions with your classmates.

1. Did you ever spend time in another country or culture?

2. What are some ideas people around the world have about your country or culture?

3. Look at the photo. Where do you think this is? What do you think the people are doing?

B Listen to *The Q Classroom* online. Then match the ideas in the box with the students.

a. We learn from them.

b. It's interesting.

c. ~~People are different.~~

d. It helps us live peacefully.

Why do we study other cultures?	
Marcus	c. People are different.
Yuna	
Felix	
Sophy	

iQ ONLINE **C** Go to the Online Discussion Board to discuss the Unit Question with your classmates.

D What are some things that make your culture different from other cultures? Write your ideas in the chart.

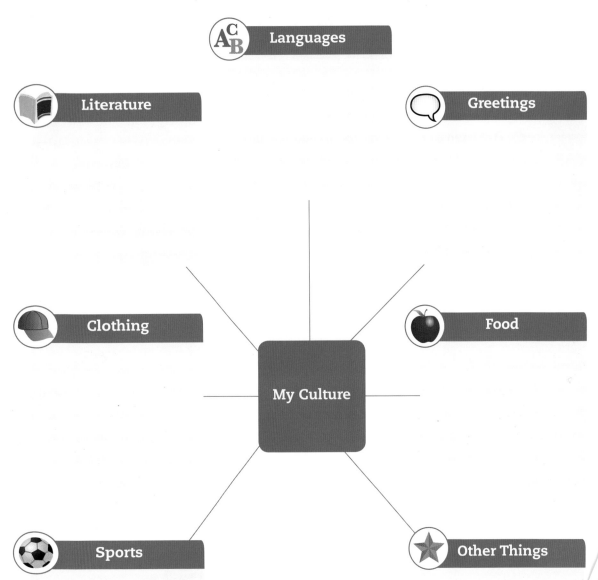

E Work in a group. Use your chart from Activity D and present one interesting fact about your culture to your group.

"In my country, people bow when they greet each other."

Taking notes in a T-chart

You can use a **T-chart** to organize your notes. In Unit 1, you organized key words and main ideas in two columns, similar to a T-chart. Now you will use a T-chart to take notes on main ideas and details. Details include examples, numbers, facts, names, and reasons. Write the main ideas on the left and the details on the right.

Read the information about culture shock from an international student handbook. Then look at a student's T-chart below.

> Spending time in a different culture can be difficult. International students may experience "culture shock." This is especially common during the first few months after they arrive in a new place. The term *culture shock* describes an uncomfortable feeling that comes from being in a new environment far from home. Signs of culture shock differ from person to person and may include feeling sad, homesick, sleepy, or angry.

Main Ideas	Details
• International students: may have culture shock	• Common during first few months
• Culture shock: uncomfortable feeling when far from home	• Signs: feeling sad, homesick, sleepy, angry

Tip for Success

To identify the main ideas, remember to listen for key words and phrases.

A. Listen to the beginning of a presentation about culture shock for new international university students. Take notes in the chart as you listen.

Main Ideas	Details

B. Compare notes with a partner.

C. Go online for more practice with taking notes in a T-chart.

LISTENING

LISTENING 1 | International Advertising

You are going to listen to a lecture from a business class at a university. The professor is talking about international advertising. As you listen to the lecture, gather information and ideas about why we study other cultures.

PREVIEW THE LISTENING

A. Here are some words from Listening 1. Read the conversations below. Then match each <u>underlined</u> word with its definition.

Tip for Success

Form a "study group" with some classmates to discuss things you learn in class.

a. when a life finishes

b. a problem

c. to try not to do something

d. something that you do that is wrong

e. something a group of people usually do

f. between different countries

g. the lowest part of something

h. thinking or talking about the good parts of a situation

Vocabulary Skill Review

In Unit 1, you learned how to distinguish between words with similar meanings. Look at the vocabulary words in Activity A. Do you know any other words with similar meanings?

____ 1. **A:** I started a job at a great company.
    B: Oh, where is it?
    A: Well, it's an <u>international</u> company. They have offices around the world.

____ 2. **A:** I lived in Europe for six months.
    B: Really? What was it like?
    A: Well, I had <u>difficulty</u> understanding the culture, but I really enjoyed it.

____ 3. **A:** I made a big <u>mistake</u> at work.
    B: Oh, no. What did you do?
    A: I called my new boss by his first name. He looked very angry.

____ 4. **A:** Do colors have different meanings in different cultures?
    B: Yes. Sometimes a color has a good or <u>positive</u> meaning in one culture and a bad meaning in another culture.

____ 5. **A:** There are different ideas around the world about <u>death</u>.
    B: What do you mean?
    A: I mean, in some countries people wear black and are very sad, but in others people celebrate.

_____ 6. A: In Korea, do people take off their shoes when they enter their
           homes?
        B: Yes, it's a Korean <u>custom</u>.

_____ 7. A: I'm going to India on business. Do you have any travel advice?
        B: Yes. <u>Avoid</u> using your left hand. For example, it's very impolite
           to shake hands or eat with your left hand.

_____ 8. A: In the Middle East, you shouldn't show the <u>bottom</u> of your shoes.
        B: Why not?
        A: Shoes are dirty. It's not polite.

iQ ONLINE **B.** Go online for more practice with the vocabulary.

C. PREVIEW You are going to listen to a university business class.
The professor is giving a lecture about international advertising
and the problems companies have when advertising in different
countries. Check (✓) the problems you think advertisers have.

☐ language mistakes
☐ problems with colors
☐ problems with numbers
☐ problems with different customs

WORK WITH THE LISTENING

A. LISTEN AND TAKE NOTES Listen to the lecture. Make a T-chart and,
in the left column, take notes on the main ideas. Use the sample notes
below to help you.

Lecture: International Advertising

Main Ideas	Details
• Language mistakes can cause problems for companies.	• Product name has funny or strange meaning in another language

B. Listen again. Add any important details in the right column of your
T-chart. Then compare notes with a partner.

C. Complete the statements about the lecture with information from the box. Use your notes to help you.

colors	lose money
international advertising	make cultural mistakes
learn about the customs	product name

1. International companies sometimes _____ in advertising.

2. Language differences can be a problem in _____.

3. A _____ may have a funny meaning in another language.

4. Some _____ are not good to use in advertisements.

5. Companies sometimes _____ because of advertising mistakes.

6. To avoid problems, companies should _____ of other countries.

D. The professor gives two examples of international advertising mistakes. Write notes to complete the chart about the mistakes.

	Type of company	Where the mistake happened	Mistake
Example 1			
Example 2			

E. Read the statements. Write _T_ (true) or _F_ (false). Correct any false statements.

___ 1. The computer company did not change the product name.

_____

___ 2. The color red usually has a positive meaning.

_____

___ 3. Companies should avoid the color blue in advertising.

_____

___ 4. The colors black and green can both mean death.

_____

F. Circle the answer that best completes each statement. Use information from the listening and your own ideas.

1. Today there are more ___ than in the past.
   a. advertising companies
   b. colors in advertising
   c. international companies

2. It is important for companies to learn about other countries' cultures ___.
   a. because they may be the same
   b. before they advertise there
   c. when they buy their products

3. When international companies understand other cultures, they ___.
   a. probably lose less money
   b. may have problems in the future
   c. don't advertise internationally

SAY WHAT YOU THINK

Discuss the questions in a group.

1. What do companies need to think about when they advertise in other countries? Give an example from your experience. Think about the problems with language, color, and customs in Listening 1.

2. What colors have special meaning in your country?

When you listen, focus on the main ideas (the most important points about the topic) and any important details. Remember that details include examples, numbers, facts, names, and reasons. Ask yourself, "What information is important for me to know?"

Lecture: International Advertising

Main Ideas	Details
• Language mistakes can cause problems for companies.	• Product name has funny or strange meaning in another language

 A. Listen to an excerpt from a lecture. Complete the T-chart with the missing information.

Lecture: International Advertising

Main Idea	Details
International companies should _____ _____	• Numbers _____ in one culture, bad in another • Some languages in _____, word for 4 _____ _____ • Ex: company put 4 _____ _____ in package, no one in _____ bought them

 B. Listen to another excerpt from a lecture. Take notes in the T-chart. Then compare notes with a partner.

Main Ideas	Details

iQ ONLINE   **C.** Go online for more practice with listening for main ideas and details.

LISTENING 2 | Cultural Problems

You are going to listen to three people talking about cultural problems. As you listen to the stories, gather information and ideas about why we study other cultures.

PREVIEW THE LISTENING

A. **VOCABULARY** Here are some words from Listening 2. Read their definitions. Then complete each sentence below with the correct word. Change the verb form if you need to.

> **carefully** (*adverb*) 🔑 a way of doing something so you don't make a mistake
>
> **confused** (*adjective*) 🔑 not able to think clearly; not understanding
>
> **die** (*verb*) 🔑 to stop living
>
> **invite** (*verb*) 🔑 to ask someone to come somewhere or to do something
>
> **offended** (*adjective*) angry or unhappy because someone does something you don't think is polite
>
> **rude** (*adjective*) 🔑 not polite
>
> **upset** (*adjective*) 🔑 unhappy or worried
>
> **wedding** (*noun*) 🔑 a special event when two people get married

🔑 Oxford 2000 keywords

1. There's a new student from Turkey in our English class.

   Let's _____ him to our house for dinner tomorrow.

2. I saw Lisa crying after class. She looked very _____.

3. Susan was an hour late, and she didn't call. Isn't that very

   _____?

4. In the Middle East, you should always say yes when someone offers you

   something. If you say no, the person may be _____.

5. In some countries, it's common to wear black when someone

   _____.

6. Colors are an important part of a _____. Many women

   wear a white dress, but in some countries, women wear red.

7. I didn't understand English well when I visited Ireland. When people spoke, I felt a little _____. But I still had a great time.

8. Watch people _____. Then you won't make a mistake.

B. Go online for more practice with the vocabulary.

C. PREVIEW You are going to listen to three people telling about cultural problems. Look at the photos. What cultural problem do you think each shows?

WORK WITH THE LISTENING

A. LISTEN AND TAKE NOTES Listen to Joao, Tanya, and Rick tell their stories. Use a T-chart to take notes on the main ideas and details of each story.

B. Compare notes with a partner.

C. Read the sentences. Then listen again. Circle the word or phrase that best completes each sentence.

1. Joao's story happened in (his home country / a store / a university class).

2. In Brazil, it is probably (rude / confusing / OK) to stand close to other people.

3. Tanya felt (positive / confused / upset) about her trip to Canada.

4. Russians often give flowers when someone (takes a trip / dies / is offended).

5. People in the United States usually use business cards when they (meet someone new / do business / take a trip).

6. Some guests at Rick's friend's wedding were probably (offended / rude / working).

D. Match the information in the box with the person.

attended a special event	is a university student in the U.S.
did not make a cultural mistake	offended someone in a shop
enjoyed meeting a friend's family	went to another country for business

Joao	
Tanya	
Rick	*attended a special event*

E. Read the questions. Then circle the correct answer.

1. Which statement is true about Joao's story?
   a. He offended a very close friend.
   b. He did not know he was rude until later.
   c. The custom is also rude in his culture.

2. Which statement describes Tanya's experience?
   a. She was upset when her coworkers gave her six flowers.
   b. She did not understand why her coworkers gave her gifts.
   c. She was not offended by the cultural mistake.

3. Which statement is true about Rick's experience?
   a. He did something that was not polite.
   b. He thought the other guests were very rude.
   c. He brought his business cards to the wedding.

4. What is true about all three people?
   a. They are all university students.
   b. They all made a cultural mistake.
   c. They all learned something important.

F. Complete the sentences with your own ideas and compare answers with a partner. Then check your answers with another pair.

1. The student at the bookstore was upset because Joao _____

    _____.

2. Joao didn't know what was wrong. He felt _____

    _____.

3. Tanya's coworkers gave her gifts because _____

    _____.

4. Tanya thinks some other Russians might _____

    _____.

5. In Russia, it's OK to _____.

6. Rick learned that in Japan, you should always _____

    _____.

iQ **ONLINE** **G.** Go online to listen to *My Grandmother* and check your comprehension.

Q ? **SAY WHAT YOU THINK**

A. Discuss the questions in a group.

1. Do you know any of the customs from Listening 2? Read each statement and check (✓) *Yes* or *No*. Then discuss your answers.

	Yes	No
1. In my culture, it's rude to stand very close to someone.	☐	☐
2. Some numbers in my culture have a special meaning.	☐	☐
3. In my culture, people only use business cards in business situations.	☐	☐

2. Do you have an example of a cultural problem? Tell your classmates the story.

B. Before you watch the video, discuss the questions in a group.

1. Think about your country and culture a long time ago. What are some things that are different now from the past?

2. What are some things that are still the same?

C. Go online to watch the video about Shanghai, China. Then check your comprehension.

VIDEO VOCABULARY

neighborhood *(n.)* a place where people live
pace *(n.)* speed
traditional *(adj.)* original; from the past
village *(n.)* a very small town

D. Think about the unit video, Listening 1, and Listening 2 as you discuss the questions.

1. What problems can happen when people don't know about another culture?

2. What are some important things people from other cultures should know about your culture?

Vocabulary Skill | Words in context

When you listen, you will sometimes hear words you don't know. You can use other information to help you guess the meaning of new words. This is called **context**. The words that come before and after another word are the context.

> Then he looked very upset and said, "Excuse me!" and moved away.
> I didn't know what was wrong. I was **confused**. I learned later that . . .

You can guess the meaning of *confused* from the context. The speaker says, "I didn't know what was wrong." *Confused* is a feeling. (The speaker says, "I was *confused*.") You can guess that *confused* is a feeling that you have when you don't understand.

A. Listen to a student's story about living in Australia. Use the context to guess the meaning. Circle the correct meaning of each word.

1. **depressed**
   (a.) very sad
   b. very offended

2. **tough**
   a. enjoyable; fun
   b. difficult or challenging

3. **considerate**
   a. caring; thoughtful
   b. rude and unkind

4. **treated**
   a. avoided
   b. behaved toward

5. **optimistic**
   a. cheerful; positive
   b. stressful and worried

Ayers Rock, Australia

B. Listen again. Write any words or phrases that helped you get the meaning. Compare answers with a partner.

1. <u>first time away, miss my family</u>

2. _____

3. _____

4. _____

5. _____

 C. Go online for more practice with words in context.

SPEAKING

 **UNIT OBJECTIVE** At the end of this unit, you are going to give a presentation about customs in a culture you know well. As you give your presentation, you will need to present information from your notes.

Grammar   Part 1 *Should* and *shouldn't*

To form a sentence, use a **subject** + ***should/shouldn't*** + **the base form of a verb.**

> I
> You
> He / She   **should** learn customs of other countries.
> We   **shouldn't** make too many cultural mistakes.
> You
> They

Note: *Shouldn't* is the contraction of *should* + *not*.

Use *should* to say that it is good to do something.

> In Japan, you **should** take a business card with two hands.

When something is <u>not</u> good to do, we use *shouldn't*.

> You **shouldn't** give six or eight flowers in Russia.

A. What do you know about customs from around the world? Circle *should* or *shouldn't*. Then listen and check your answers.

1. In India, you (should / shouldn't) use your left hand to eat.

2. In Vietnam, you (should / shouldn't) touch a person on the head.

3. In the U.S., you (should / shouldn't) look at people's eyes when you speak to them.

4. In France, when you visit someone's home, you (should / shouldn't) bring a gift.

5. In Saudi Arabia, you (should / shouldn't) say no when someone offers you something to eat or drink.

6. In Colombia, you (should / shouldn't) avoid giving marigolds—a yellow flower—as a gift.

B. What are things you should or shouldn't do in your culture? Write two sentences with *should* and two sentences with *shouldn't*. Then read your sentences to a partner.

1. _____

2. _____

3. _____

4. _____

Grammar   Part 2 It's + adjective + infinitive

You can make statements with ***it's*** + (***not***) **adjective** + **infinitive** to talk about behavior and customs. The infinitive is ***to*** + the base form of a verb.

> **It's polite to say** "thank you."
> **It's rude to show** the bottom of your feet.
> **It's common to wear** a white wedding dress.
> **It's not common to wear** a green wedding dress.
> **It's OK to use** your first name.
> **It's not OK to use** your short name.

Note: *It's* is the contraction of *it* + *is*.

 A. Listen to the excerpts from Listening 2. Fill in the blanks with the missing information.

1. There was another student standing in front of the shelf. I stood next to him and started to look for my book. Then he looked very upset and said, "Excuse me!" and moved away. I didn't know what was wrong. I was confused. I learned later that you shouldn't stand very close to other people in the U.S. _____.

2. They gave me some very nice gifts . . . and they gave me flowers—six flowers. In Russia, _____ of flowers, for example, one, three, five. . . . But you shouldn't give two, four, or six flowers. We only do that when a person dies.

3. I was a little surprised. In the U.S., we only use cards for business, so I didn't bring mine. I just took the Japanese people's business cards and put them in my pocket. After the wedding, I learned that _____. You should always take the cards with two hands and read them carefully. I only used one hand, and I didn't read them at all!

B. What are customs in your culture or another culture you know? Write one sentence for each topic in the box. Use *it's* + (*not*) adjective + infinitive.

eating/drinking	greetings	visiting someone's home
gestures	holidays	workplace/office

1. _____

2. _____

3. _____

4. _____

5. _____

6. _____

C. Work in a group. Take turns reading your sentences. Ask questions if you don't understand.

D. Go online for more practice with *should* and *shouldn't* and *it's* + adjective + infinitive.

E. Go online for the grammar expansion.

Pronunciation   The schwa /ə/ sound

The **schwa** /ə/ is the most common vowel sound in English. It sounds like the *a* in *about* /əˈbaʊt/. We pronounce the vowel in many unstressed syllables (or parts of words) with the schwa /ə/ sound. The schwa /ə/ is never in a stressed syllable.

In these examples, the vowels in red are pronounced with a schwa /ə/ sound.

avoid	cultural	custom	international	problem

A. Listen and repeat these words. Then <u>underline</u> the schwa sound in each word.

1. <u>a</u>void
2. bottom
3. considerate
4. offended
5. personality
6. positive
7. similar
8. telephone

B. Write four sentences. In each sentence, use a word from Activity A. Then take turns reading your sentences with a partner.

1. _____

2. _____

3. _____

4. _____

iQ ONLINE **C.** Go online for more practice with the schwa /ə/ sound.

Speaking Skill | Presenting information from notes

When you present information to an audience, you should not read directly from your notes. It's important to look up and make eye contact with the audience. This makes the presentation more interesting.

Preparation

- Use small cards.
- Write only key words and phrases. Don't write the whole presentation.
- Practice your presentation.

Presentation

- Look at the audience. Then begin speaking.
- Look down briefly to check your notes.
- Make eye contact with individual people in your audience as you speak.

Tip for Success

Before you give a presentation, practice it several times. Try standing in front of a mirror. Practice speaking from notes and making eye contact until you feel comfortable.

A. Read the Web page with tips for visiting Egypt. <u>Underline</u> the key words and phrases for each tip.

EGYPT
EXPLORE. DISCOVER. EXPERIENCE.

| Experience Egypt | **Culture Tips for Travelers** | Sights and Activities | Organize your trip | 🔍 |

Culture Tips for Travelers

EATING
- ▲ You should only use your right hand for eating. It's impolite to use the left hand. Your host may be offended.
- ▲ When you finish eating, your host will offer more food. Even if you are not hungry, you should take a little more. It's important to show that you enjoy the meal.

VISITING SOMEONE'S HOME
- ▲ You should always dress neatly and conservatively when you visit someone's home.
- ▲ It's common to bring a gift for the host. You should bring chocolates or other sweets. It isn't good to bring flowers because it's common to bring flowers when someone is sick.

GIFT-GIVING
- ▲ You should receive a gift with the right hand or both hands. You shouldn't use the left hand.
- ▲ You shouldn't open the gift when someone gives it to you. It's polite to wait until later.

Some Useful Words
- ▶ Hello
- ▶ How are you?
- ▶ Can you help me?

Getting Directions

Getting Around

Shopping

Flowers of Egypt

B. Complete the notes with the key words and phrases from the web page.

Culture Tips for Visiting Egypt Presentation Notes

1. _____ Eating _____

   - only use _____ your right hand _____

   - impolite to use _____

   - host will _____ ;

     you should _____

2. _____ someone's home

   - _____ and conservatively

   - bring _____ ,

     such as _____

   - do NOT bring _____

3. _____

   - receive a gift _____

   - do NOT use _____

   - should wait to _____

C. Work with a partner. Take turns presenting the information in Activity B. Be sure to look at your partner when you speak.

iQ ONLINE **D.** Go online for more practice with presenting information from notes.

In this assignment, you are going to plan and give a presentation about your culture or another culture you know well. As you prepare your presentation, think about the Unit Question, "Why do we study other cultures?" Use information from Listening 1, Listening 2, the unit video, and your work in the unit to support your presentation. Refer to the Self-Assessment checklist on page 48.

CONSIDER THE IDEAS

Look again at the web page on page 45. Discuss these questions in a group.

1. Are any of the customs in Egypt similar to customs you know? Which ones?

2. Do you think it's important to learn the customs of a country you visit? Why or why not?

PREPARE AND SPEAK

A. GATHER IDEAS Choose three topics from the box and write them in the T-chart below. Complete the T-chart with notes about customs in your culture or another culture you know well.

business	gestures	greetings
eating and drinking	gift-giving	visiting someone's home

Topic	Customs
1.	
2.	
3.	

Critical Thinking **Tip**

In Activity B, you are going to **prepare** your presentation. **Preparing** a presentation on a topic involves applying your knowledge in a new way or doing something new.

B. ORGANIZE IDEAS Use your notes from the T-chart in Activity A to prepare a short presentation about customs in your culture or another culture you know well. Write your presentation notes on note cards.

C. SPEAK Give your presentation to the class (or to a group). Use your note cards during the presentation, and remember to look at your audience. Refer to the Self-Assessment checklist below before you begin.

 Go online for your alternate Unit Assignment.

CHECK AND REFLECT

A. CHECK Think about the Unit Assignment as you complete the Self-Assessment checklist.

SELF-ASSESSMENT		
Yes	**No**	
☐	☐	I was able to speak easily about the topic.
☐	☐	I used a T-chart to take notes on main ideas and details.
☐	☐	My partner/group/class understood me.
☐	☐	I used *should/shouldn't* and *it's* + (*not*) adjective + infinitive correctly.
☐	☐	I used vocabulary from the unit.
☐	☐	I presented information from notes.
☐	☐	I correctly pronounced any words with schwa /ə/.

 B. REFLECT Go to the Online Discussion Board to discuss these questions.

1. What is something new you learned in this unit?

2. Look back at the Unit Question—Why do we study other cultures? Is your answer different now than when you started the unit? If yes, how is it different? Why?

TRACK YOUR SUCCESS

Circle the words you have learned in this unit.

Nouns	Verbs	
bottom 🔑	avoid 🔑	international 🔑
custom 🔑	die 🔑	offended
death 🔑	invite 🔑	optimistic
difficulty 🔑	treat 🔑	positive 🔑 AWL
mistake 🔑		rude 🔑
wedding 🔑	**Adjectives**	tough
	confused 🔑	upset 🔑
	considerate	
	depressed AWL	**Adverb**
		carefully 🔑

🔑 Oxford 2000 keywords

AWL Academic Word List

Check (✓) the skills you learned. If you need more work on a skill, refer to the page(s) in parentheses.

NOTE TAKING ■	I can take notes in a T-chart. (p. 29)
LISTENING ■	I can listen for main ideas and details. (p. 34)
VOCABULARY ■	I can guess meaning from context. (p. 39)
GRAMMAR ■	I can understand and use *should/shouldn't* and *it's* + (*not*) adjective + infinitive. (pp. 41 and 42)
PRONUNCIATION ■	I can recognize and pronounce the schwa /ə/ sound. (p. 43)
SPEAKING ■	I can present information from notes. (p. 44)
UNIT OBJECTIVE ▶▶▶▶ ■	I can gather information and ideas to give a presentation about customs in a culture I know well.

NOTE TAKING ▶	marking important information in notes
LISTENING ▶	understanding numbers and dates
VOCABULARY ▶	suffixes *-ful* and *-ing*
GRAMMAR ▶	*be going to*
PRONUNCIATION ▶	reduction of *be going to*
SPEAKING ▶	introducing topics in a presentation

UNIT QUESTION

What is the best kind of vacation?

A Discuss these questions with your classmates.

1. What did you do on your last vacation?

2. What are popular places for tourists in your home country?

3. Look at the photo. Where are these people? Is this the kind of vacation you would go on?

B Listen to *The Q Classroom* online. Then answer these questions.

1. Yuna says she prefers a relaxing beach vacation. What kinds of vacations do Sophy and Felix prefer?

2. Which student's opinion do you agree with? Why?

iQ ONLINE **C** Go online to watch the video about popular tourist places. Then check your comprehension.

VIDEO VOCABULARY

lifetime *(n.)* a person's entire life

market *(n.)* a place where people buy food, clothing, or other goods

tourist attraction *(n.)* a place where many people come to visit

iQ ONLINE **D** Go to the Online Discussion Board to discuss the Unit Question with your classmates.

E Work with a partner. Look at each sign. What does it mean? What are some locations where you might see it?

Meaning: _____

_____

Locations: _____

_____

Meaning: _____

_____

Locations: _____

_____

Meaning: _____

_____

Locations: _____

_____

Meaning: _____

_____

Locations: _____

_____

Meaning: _____

_____

Locations: _____

_____

Meaning: _____

_____

Locations: _____

_____

F Look again at the signs in Activity E. Discuss these questions in a group.

1. Why do you think the signs were put up?

2. Do you think people need signs like these? Why or why not?

3. Can you think of examples of similar signs? Draw or explain one to your group.

When you take notes, it is helpful to mark specific details or information. For example, you can underline, box, circle, or star (✳) important facts, names, numbers, or dates. This will make it easy to find and remember the information in your notes later.

You can also use **symbols** to mark your feelings as you take notes. For example, use an exclamation point (!) for a surprising fact or a question mark (?) for something you don't understand. You can check your questions later and add to your notes.

 Listen to the beginning of a lecture about Costa Rica. Read the student's notes and notice the marking.

> *Lecture: Costa Rica*
> *Located in (Central America)*
> *Borders <u>Nicaragua</u>, <u>Panama</u>, <u>Pacific Ocean</u>,*
> *<u>Caribbean Sea</u>*
> *16th-18th centuries – Spanish rule✳*
> *Independent country – Sept. 21, 1821*
> *Popular for tourists = 2 million/year!*

A. Listen to the next part of the presentation about Costa Rica. Take notes as you listen.

B. Look at your notes and mark the important information with symbols. Then compare notes with a partner.

 **C.** Go online for more practice with marking important information in notes.

LISTENING

LISTENING 1 | Places in Danger

UNIT OBJECTIVE

You are going to listen to a report from a travel program. As you listen to the report, gather information and ideas about what the best kind of vacation is.

PREVIEW THE LISTENING

A. **VOCABULARY** Here are some words from Listening 1. Read their definitions. Then complete each sentence below with the correct word. Change nouns to plural if you need to.

> **Tip** for Success
>
> Pay attention to the listening title. Think about it before you start listening. Ask yourself, *What is this about? What do I know about this topic?*

---

dangerous (*adjective*) 🔑 may hurt you

destroy (*verb*) 🔑 to break or ruin something

insect (*noun*) 🔑 a small animal with six legs, such as an ant or a fly

local (*adjective*) 🔑 of a place near you

pollution (*noun*) 🔑 dirty air or water

shake (*verb*) 🔑 to move quickly up and down or from side to side

tourist (*noun*) 🔑 a person who visits a place on vacation

🔑 Oxford 2000 keywords

1. If you travel to Mexico, you should try the _____ food. Tacos are my favorite dish.

2. Suddenly, the building started to _____. We all ran outside.

3. Too many visitors could _____ these very old houses.

4. Many big cities have problems with _____. Cars and buses make the air dirty.

5. Many countries need _____ to help the local economy.

6. Do you think it's _____ to travel alone?

7. What kind of _____ is that? It's such a colorful bug.

iQ ONLINE **B.** Go online for more practice with the vocabulary.

C. **PREVIEW** You are going to listen to a report from a travel program called *Places in Danger*. The program talks about the negative effects of tourists visiting three famous places. Look at these places. What do you know about them? Why do you think they are in danger?

1

the Great Wall of China

2

the Galapagos Islands, Ecuador

3

Antarctica

WORK WITH THE LISTENING

A. **LISTEN AND TAKE NOTES** Listen to the presentation. Take notes on the effects of tourism in each of the three places: the Great Wall of China, the Galapagos Islands, and Antarctica. Use the example below to guide you.

Great Wall	Galapagos Islands	Antarctica
runs across	in Pacific Ocean,	first tourists – 1956
north of China	near S. America	

B. Look at your notes. Mark the important information. Follow the examples of marking and symbols on page 53. Then compare notes with a partner.

C. Listen again. What problems do tourists cause at each place? Fill in the blanks with the missing information.

	Problems caused by tourists
Great Wall of China	Millions of _____ _____. Buses and cars _____.
Galapagos Islands	Planes and boats sometimes _____.
Antarctica	Tourist business causes _____, changes _____, and causes problems for _____.

D. Look at these signs. Where would tourists see them: at the Great Wall of China, the Galapagos Islands, or Antarctica? Write the name of the place under each sign.

_____   _____   _____

E. Listen again. Complete the sentences that explain what people are doing to protect each place.

1. Great Wall of China: Many areas _____.

2. Galapagos Islands: Airlines must _____

   _____.

3. Antarctica: Tourists cannot _____.

   They cannot move or take _____.

   They must wash _____.

F. Read the statements. Write *T* (true) or *F* (false). Then correct any false statements.

____ 1. The Great Wall is open to visitors every day.

   _____

____ 2. Tourists drive cars and buses on top of the Great Wall.

   _____

____ 3. Of all three places, the Great Wall gets the most visitors each year.

   _____

____ 4. The Galapagos Islands are home to thousands of people.

   _____

_____ 5. The number of tourists to Antarctica is growing.

SAY WHAT YOU THINK

Discuss the questions in a group.

1. Were you surprised about the problems at these places? Why or why not?

2. Think of one more idea to help each place. Then share it with the class.

3. Name some famous places in your country. Do tourists cause any problems there?

| Listening Skill | Understanding numbers and dates |

It's important to understand numbers when you listen; for example, when you listen to detailed information on a TV or radio program or during a lecture.

Numbers ending in *-teen* or *-ty* can be difficult. You need to listen carefully for the stress patterns in these numbers. That way you can be sure you understand the numbers correctly.

- **In numbers ending in *-ty*,** the first syllable is stressed: FIF-ty.
- **In numbers ending in *-teen*,** the stress is on the last syllable: fif-TEEN.

Listen to these pairs of numbers.

14 / 40   15 / 50   16 / 60   17 / 70   18 / 80   19 / 90

Listen to these large numbers.

453	four hundred fifty-three
3,227	three thousand two hundred twenty-seven
15,609	fifteen thousand six hundred nine
275,000	two hundred seventy-five thousand
8,250,000	eight million two hundred fifty thousand

Listen to these dates.

1700 → seventeen hundred   1989 → nineteen eighty-nine
1809 → eighteen oh nine   2011 → twenty eleven (two thousand eleven)

A. Listen to excerpts from Listening 1. Complete the student's notes
below with the missing information.

Great Wall of China	Runs _____ kilometers across north
	Some parts over _____ years old
	About _____ tourists/day
	(_____ visitors/year)
Galapagos Islands	_____ main islands – home to thousands of plants and animals
	About _____ tourists/year
Antarctica	First tourists arrived in _____
	Only about _____ visitors/year
	then Today, close to _____

B. Mark the important information and details in the notes. Then compare
notes with a partner.

C. Complete the travel quiz with a partner. Then listen and check your answers.

What do you know about the world?
Take this travel quiz, and find out!

1. Mount Everest is ____ meters high.
   a. 850
   b. 8,850
   c. 9,580

2. The Eiffel Tower in Paris was built in ____.
   a. 1599
   b. 1702
   c. 1889

3. Burj Khalifa, the tallest building in the world, is ____ meters tall.
   a. 828
   b. 880
   c. 8,018

4. The population of New York City is about ____.
   a. 83,000
   b. 8,300,000
   c. 63,000,000

5. There are ____ islands in the Philippines.
   a. 717
   b. 7,107
   c. 71,000

6. Angel Falls in Venezuela is the world's tallest waterfall. It's ____ meters tall.
   a. 979
   b. 1,065
   c. 2,500

A: I think Mount Everest is 8,850 meters high. What do you think?

B: I'm not sure. Maybe it's nine thousand . . .

 D. Go online for more practice with understanding numbers and dates.

LISTENING 2 | A Helpful Vacation

UNIT OBJECTIVE ▶▶▶▶
You are going to listen to the owner of a travel company give a presentation about jobs for volunteers in Cusco, Peru. As you listen to the presentation, gather information and ideas about what the best kind of vacation is.

PREVIEW THE LISTENING

Vocabulary Skill Review

In Unit 2, you learned about finding the meaning of new words through the context. Try to find the meaning of the vocabulary words in Activity A by looking at the context.

A. **VOCABULARY** Here are some words from Listening 2. Read the sentences. Circle the answer that best matches the meaning of each underlined word.

1. After college, Yolanda wants to work as a <u>volunteer</u>.
   a. someone who works without pay   b. someone who does difficult work

2. We really enjoyed our trip to Europe. We saw lots of <u>pretty</u> towns and took some great pictures.
   a. dangerous   b. beautiful

3. China has the largest <u>population</u> of all the world's countries. In some cities, you could have millions of "neighbors"!
   a. number of people   b. number of buildings

4. The Mada'in Saleh is an <u>ancient</u> site. No one knows exactly who built it.
   a. very small   b. very old

5. I'm going to Morocco tomorrow, so I have to pack my bags and <u>prepare</u> for my trip.
   a. get ready   b. get tired

6. We waited in the airport for a long time. There was a problem with the airplane and they had to <u>repair</u> it.
   a. fix   b. destroy

7. In the summer, I work as a tour guide. I <u>lead</u> tourists to interesting places in my hometown.
   a. take   b. shake

8. I love to travel and learn about different cultures. It's very <u>enjoyable</u>.
   a. not fun   b. fun

iQ ONLINE **B.** Go online for more practice with the vocabulary.

C. **PREVIEW** Volunteer Vacations is a travel company that offers work and travel around the world. You are going to listen to the owner of the company giving a presentation about jobs for volunteers in Cusco, Peru.

Look at the pictures. Check (✓) the activities you think the volunteers will do.

1

visit Machu Picchu

2

paint a school

3

volunteer as a teacher

4

go to a Peruvian beach

WORK WITH THE LISTENING

A. **LISTEN AND TAKE NOTES** Listen to the presentation and complete the student's notes.

Cusco – population _____, near Andes Mountains

_____ hours by train to Machu Picchu ✳ (visit end of first week!)

Trip is from June _____ to July _____

Live with _____

Volunteer work: help _____, may _____ English!

B. Compare notes with a partner. Listen again and correct any errors in your notes.

C. Each of these statements is false. Correct them.

1. Cusco, Peru is a small town near the Andes Mountains.

   _____

2. The volunteers will visit Machu Picchu after four weeks.

   _____

3. The volunteers will travel to Peru during April and May.

   _____

4. The group will live at a local school.

   _____

5. For work, the volunteers will repair houses.

   _____

6. They may teach Spanish to children at a school.

   _____

D. Match the sentence halves to form true statements.

____ 1. Machu Picchu is a good place to

____ 2. During the first two weeks the group will

____ 3. The main goal of the volunteers is to

____ 4. The volunteers may

a. study the language and culture of Peru.

b. learn about ancient history.

c. teach their own language.

d. help the local people.

E. Read the sentences. Then check (✓) *True* or *False*. If the information is not in the presentation, check *It doesn't say*.

	True	False	It doesn't say.
1. All of the volunteers are university students.	☐	☐	☐
2. The volunteer work will begin the first week.	☐	☐	☐
3. Some of the host families can speak English.	☐	☐	☐
4. The volunteers will work in a new school.	☐	☐	☐
5. This is the travel company's first trip to a school.	☐	☐	☐

F. Compare answers with a partner. Correct any false statements.

G. Go online to listen to *The Peace Boat* and check your comprehension.

SAY WHAT YOU THINK

A. Discuss the questions in a group.

1. Do you think this volunteer tour sounds like an exciting vacation? Why or why not?

2. Do you want to take a volunteer tour? Where do you want to go?

3. How can you help in another place?

B. Think about the unit video, Listening 1, and Listening 2 as you discuss the questions.

1. What are some of the good and bad effects of tourists visiting famous places? Add more good and bad effects to the T-chart below.

Good	Bad
brings money to local people	causes pollution

2. What activities can volunteers do to help the people in your country or where you live?

Suffixes are letters or groups of letters at the end of a word. Suffixes can change the tense (-*ed*, -*ing*), the number (-*s*, -*es*), or the part of speech of a word. Learning different suffixes is a good way to build your vocabulary.

• The suffix -*ful* changes a noun to an adjective.

> beauty → beautiful   The Burj Al Arab is a **beautiful** building.
> wonder → wonderful   The restaurants in Dubai are **wonderful**.

• The suffix -*ing* can change a verb to an adjective.

> excite → exciting   Tokyo is an **exciting** place. There are many fun things to do.
> interest → interesting   Our visit to Machu Picchu was very **interesting**.

A. Read the sentences. Write the adjective form of each word in parentheses.

1. If you go to Peru, you should visit Machu Picchu. The old stone

   buildings are _____ (amaze).

2. Until about 1920, the Galapagos Islands were very _____

   (peace). Only animals lived there, no people.

3. Sometimes tourists can be _____ (help) to the place they

   visit. They create jobs for local people.

4. We visited Venice, Italy during our last vacation. It is a very

   _____ (charm) city.

5. I don't want to just go to the beach for my vacation. I want to do

   something _____ (meaning), like volunteer work.

6. The Great Wall of China is in danger because of the _____

   (rise) number of tourists.

7. Did you enjoy your volunteer tour? I want to take one next year. I heard

   it's a very _____ (interest) experience.

8. Many areas of the Great Wall of China are now closed to visitors.

   It's very fragile, so you have to be _____ (care).

B. Write four sentences about a tourist place you visited. Use the words to form adjectives with *-ing* or *-ful*.

1. _____
(wonder)

2. _____
(amaze)

3. _____
(excite)

4. _____
(beauty)

C. Share your sentences with a partner. Ask follow-up questions about the vacations or places.

A: *Beijing is a wonderful city.*
B: *Oh, when did you go there?*
A: *Last summer. It was hot there.*

A view of downtown Beijing, China

 D. Go online for more practice with the suffixes *-ful* and *-ing*.

SPEAKING

UNIT OBJECTIVE ▶▶▶▶ At the end of this unit, you are going to work in a group to plan and present a travel tour. As you give your presentation, you will need to introduce topics.

Grammar   *Be going to*

Be going to statements

We use ***be going to*** + **the base form of a verb** to talk about the future, usually about our future plans.

> Tomorrow we**'re going to visit** the Great Wall of China.
> I**'m going to take** a volunteer tour this summer.

- To form the future with *be going to*, use *am*, *is*, or *are* + *going to* + the base form of the verb.

> She **is going to study** Spanish for two weeks.
> They **are going to repair** a school in Peru.

- To make a negative statement, use *not* before *going to*.

> I **am not going to stay** in a hotel.
> We **are not going to go** shopping today.

- In speaking and informal writing, we often use contractions.

> John**'s going to fly** to the Galapagos Islands in the morning.
> The museum **isn't going to be** open tomorrow.

Be going to questions

- Form *yes/no* questions by changing the order of the subject and *be*.

> **They are going to** volunteer in Peru.
> **Are they going to** volunteer in Peru?

- Form information questions by adding the *wh-* word and changing the order of the subject and *be*.

> **Where are they going to** volunteer?

A. Read the email about a tree-planting tour in Nepal. Complete the sentences with the correct form of *be going to* and the verbs in parentheses. Use contractions.

To: ken_fujiwaka@getmail.com

From: jon.miller22@greatmail.com

Subject: Summer plans

Hi Ken,

I'm writing to tell you about my exciting summer plans. ___I'm going to join___ a
1. (join)
volunteer tour to Nepal! Here are some of the things we _____.
2. (do)
On the first day we _____ a bus to Gorkha, the old capital of
3. (take)
Nepal. It _____ a long trip—five hours! I hope it doesn't rain.
4. (be)
The tour website says that on a clear day, you can see Mount Everest from

the bus window! We _____ three days hiking and camping in
5. (spend)
the Himalayas. Our guide _____ us about the mountain plants
6. (teach)
and animals. Then our group _____ in a small town and help
7. (stop)
the local people plant trees. I think that _____ the most
8. (be)
enjoyable part of the trip. Well, I have to go.

I _____ a blog, so you can
9. (write)
read all about the trip!

Take care,

Jon

B. Match the questions with the answers. Then listen to the conversations and check your answers.

_____ 1. What are you going to do in China?

a. No, we're going to go shopping.

_____ 2. Where are we going to stay?

b. Yes, he's going to go to Hawaii.

_____ 3. Can we go to the National Museum today?

c. We're going to return on May 16th.

_____ 4. How long is your trip?

d. You're going to live with a local family.

_____ 5. Is John going to take a vacation this year?

e. I'm going to do volunteer work in Shanghai.

C. Write questions. Use _be going to_. Then ask and answer the questions with a partner.

1. What/you/do this weekend

   What are you going to do this weekend ?

2. you/study English/this weekend

   _____ ?

3. What/you/do/during the next holiday

   _____ ?

4. Where/you/travel/next summer?

   _____ ?

D. Go online for more practice with _be going to_.

E. Go online for the grammar expansion.

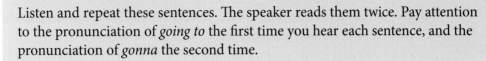

When using *be going to*, speakers, especially in the United States, often pronounce *going to* as *gonna*. They reduce the sounds.

Listen and repeat these sentences. The speaker reads them twice. Pay attention to the pronunciation of *going to* the first time you hear each sentence, and the pronunciation of *gonna* the second time.

1. We're going to visit Italy next year.
2. She isn't going to come with us.
3. I'm going to stay with a family in Madrid.
4. They aren't going to join a tour.

Note: We never write *gonna* in academic or professional writing.

A. Write answers to the questions. Use *be going to*. Then take turns asking and answering the questions with a partner. Use the reduced pronunciation of *going to*.

1. A: When are you going to take your next vacation?

   B: _____.

2. A: Where are you going to go?

   B: _____.

3. A: Who are you going to travel with?

   B: _____.

4. A: What are you going to do there?

   B: _____.

B. Imagine you are going to take a volunteer tour. Use the questions in Activity A to plan your trip. Ask and answer the questions about your trip with your partner.

iQ ONLINE **C.** Go online for more practice with the reduction of *be going to*.

When you give a presentation, you want it to be organized so that your audience can follow what you are saying. Here are some useful phrases for organizing a presentation.

- To introduce the first topic:

  Let's start with . . .
  The first thing I'm going to talk about is . . .

- To change to a new topic:

  Now let's move on to . . .
  Next, I'm going to talk about . . .

- To introduce the last topic:

  Finally, let's talk about . . .
  To wrap up, I'm going to tell you about . . .

- To introduce the next speaker (when there is more than one):

  Now Pamela is going to tell you about . . .
  Now Jun Ho is going to take over.

Critical Thinking (Tip)

Activity A asks you to **decide** on the best order. You decide by looking at everything you know about a subject. **Deciding** helps you put information together in a useful way.

A. Work with a partner. Imagine you work for a tour company. You are going to present a tour to a group of tourists. Decide on the best order to present these topics. Number them 1 to 6.

____ the cost of the trip

____ the first day

____ the flight information

____ the food

____ the schedule of places to visit

____ the volunteer activities

B. Take turns with your partner making sentences from the phrases in the Speaking Skill box above and the topics in Activity A. Follow the order you decided on in Activity A.

"The first thing I'm going to talk about is the schedule. . . ."

iQ ONLINE **C. Go online for more practice with introducing topics in a presentation.**

UNIT OBJECTIVE ▶▶▶▶ In this assignment, you are going to work in a group to plan a vacation for tourists and then present the tour to your class. As you prepare your presentation, think about the Unit Question, "What is the best kind of vacation?" Use information from Listening 1, Listening 2, the unit video, and your work in the unit to support your presentation. Refer to the Self-Assessment checklist on page 72.

CONSIDER THE IDEAS

A. Listen to two tour guides present information about a tour to Nepal. Number the topics in order.

____ activities

____ cost

____ food

____ lodging

____ schedule

B. Listen again and take notes on the details for each topic in Activity A. Then compare notes with a partner.

PREPARE AND SPEAK

A. **GATHER IDEAS** Work in a group. Imagine you work for a tour company.

1. Choose a travel destination and plan a tour to that place. Think of a place you know well or do some research on a new destination.

2. Take notes including information on schedule, lodging, food, activities, and cost.

Tip for Success

Here are some useful phrases for adding information when a co-presenter is speaking: *May I say one more thing? / I'd like to add one point. / Can I add something?*

B. **ORGANIZE IDEAS** With your group, plan a presentation to give information about your tour. Plan to use visuals such as a poster or photos in your presentation. Decide who will talk about each topic. Use your notes from Activity A.

C. **SPEAK** Practice your presentation. Then give your presentation to the class (or to a group). Refer to the Self-Assessment checklist below before you begin.

Go online for your alternate Unit Assignment.

CHECK AND REFLECT

A. CHECK Think about the Unit Assignment as you complete the Self-Assessment checklist.

SELF-ASSESSMENT		
Yes	No	
☐	☐	I was able to speak easily about the topic.
☐	☐	I marked important information in my notes.
☐	☐	My partner/group/class understood me.
☐	☐	I used *be going to* correctly.
☐	☐	I used vocabulary from the unit.
☐	☐	I introduced topics in a presentation.
☐	☐	I pronounced *be going to* correctly.

 B. REFLECT Go to the Online Discussion Board to discuss these questions.

1. What is something new you learned in this unit?

2. Think about the Unit Question—What is the best kind of vacation? Is your answer different now than when you started the unit? If yes, how is it different? Why?

TRACK YOUR SUCCESS

Circle the words and phrases you have learned in this unit.

Nouns
insect 🔑
pollution 🔑
population
tourist 🔑
volunteer AWL

Verbs
destroy 🔑
lead 🔑
prepare 🔑
repair 🔑
shake 🔑

Adjectives
ancient 🔑
dangerous 🔑
enjoyable 🔑
local 🔑
pretty 🔑

Phrases
Let's start with . . .
The first thing I'm going
    to talk about is . . .
Now let's move on to . . .
Next, I'm going
    to talk about . . .
Now (name) is going to
    tell you about . . .
Now (name) is going to
    take over.
Finally, let's talk
    about . . .
To wrap up, I'm going to
    tell you about . . .

🔑 Oxford 2000 keywords
AWL Academic Word List

Check (✓) the skills you learned. If you need more work on a skill, refer to the page(s) in parentheses.

NOTE TAKING	■	I can mark important information in notes. (p. 53)
LISTENING	■	I can understand numbers and dates. (p. 57)
VOCABULARY	■	I can recognize and use the suffixes -ful and -ing. (p. 64)
GRAMMAR	■	I can recognize and use be going to. (p. 66)
PRONUNCIATION	■	I can recognize and use the reduced pronunciation of be going to. (p. 69)
SPEAKING	■	I can introduce topics in a presentation. (p. 70)
UNIT OBJECTIVE ▶▶▶	■	I can gather information and ideas to participate in a presentation describing a travel tour.

UNIT 4

Physiology

LISTENING	▶	listening for specific information
NOTE TAKING	▶	making notes using a word web
VOCABULARY	▶	synonyms
GRAMMAR	▶	simple present for informal narratives
PRONUNCIATION	▶	simple present third-person -s / -es
SPEAKING	▶	using eye contact, tone of voice, and pause

UNIT QUESTION

Who makes you laugh?

A Discuss these questions with your classmates.

1. What funny TV shows do you like?

2. Do you tell jokes or make other people laugh?

3. Look at the photo. What are these people doing?

B Listen to *The Q Classroom* online. Then answer these questions.

1. What types of comedy or comedians do the students talk about?

2. Have you ever seen live comedy? If so, describe it.

3. Do you watch TV shows from another culture or in English or another language? Explain why you think they are funny or not funny.

iQ ONLINE **C** Go to the Online Discussion Board to discuss the Unit Question with your classmates.

D Look at the photo. The group is laughing at something they see on the laptop. What are possible reasons they are laughing? Write your ideas. Then discuss them with a partner.

_____

_____

_____

_____

A: _I think they are laughing at a new YouTube video._

B: _I think they are looking at someone's childhood pictures._

E Look at the chart. Write your answers. Then, with your partner, take turns asking for and giving information from the chart. Write your partner's answers in the chart.

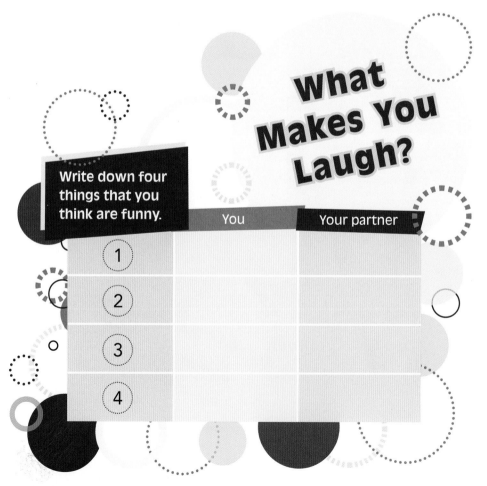

What Makes You Laugh?

Write down four things that you think are funny.	You	Your partner
1		
2		
3		
4		

LISTENING

LISTENING 1 | ## Charles Dickens—Making Readers Laugh After 200 Years

UNIT OBJECTIVE ▶▶▶ You are going to listen to a radio show about the famous British author Charles Dickens. As you listen to the program, gather information and ideas about who makes you laugh.

PREVIEW THE LISTENING

A. **VOCABULARY** Here are some words from Listening 1. Read the sentences. Then write each underlined word next to the correct definition.

1. Mark Twain wrote <u>comical</u> stories, such as *Tom Sawyer* and *Huckleberry Finn*.

2. I think John will write a book someday. He is a very <u>talented</u> writer.

3. My boss has a great <u>sense of humor</u>. She makes everyone laugh.

4. Angelina is taking a writing course. She wants to be a <u>professional</u> writer someday.

5. That TV show was popular in the United States. <u>However</u>, it was not successful in other parts of the world.

6. That new TV show is a big <u>hit</u>. Lots of people watch it.

7. Kim told me a great story. She can <u>describe</u> things in a very funny way.

8. The Smiths' new house is <u>huge</u>. It has ten bedrooms!

a. _____ (*noun*) the ability to laugh at things and think they are funny

b. _____ (*adverb*) but

c. _____ (*adjective*) very big

d. _____ (*adjective*) doing something for money as a job

e. _____ (*adjective*) funny

f. _____ (*adjective*) able to do something well

g. _____ (*noun*) a person or thing that a lot of people like

h. _____ (*verb*) to explain

B. Go online for more practice with the vocabulary.

C. PREVIEW You are going to listen to a radio show about British writer Charles Dickens. What do you think makes Dickens's books funny?

The Old Curiosity Shop

Great Expectations

WORK WITH THE LISTENING

A. LISTEN AND TAKE NOTES Listen and number the topics in the order the speaker talks about them. There are two topics you will not use.

Tip for Success

Photos can help you predict the topic and main ideas of a listening.

____ a. schooling

_____

____ b. family

_____

____ c. first professional writing job

_____

____ d. university

_____

____ e. characters

_____

____ f. birthplace

_____

B. Listen again. On the lines in Activity A, write key words and phrases about the topics.

C. Circle the answer that best completes each statement.

1. People think Dickens's books are funny because ____.
   a. the stories and people are unusual
   b. Dickens's style of writing is old
   c. they are about funny events in history

2. Many of Dickens's characters ____.
   a. have the same names as his family members
   b. are similar to real people
   c. are from the southeast part of England

3. Dickens learned to be a writer ____.
   a. when he attended college
   b. because he had a difficult life growing up
   c. working for *Pickwick Papers Magazine*

4. Dickens's stories are often about the lives of ____.
   a. sad people
   b. poor people
   c. comical people

5. Dickens was very good at ____.
   a. having interesting conversations
   b. telling very sad stories
   c. making characters seem real

D. Circle the correct information to complete each sentence.

1. As a young boy, Dickens spent a lot of time (playing with friends outdoors / traveling around the country / reading).

2. Dickens had to leave school because he did not have enough (time / money / talent).

3. When Dickens was a boy, he had to work in a shoe polish factory because (he wanted to save a lot of money / his father had money problems / he wanted to publish his books).

4. Dickens's first novel was (not very popular / a big success / only sold in London).

 | Listening and Speaking   **79**

E. Use words from the box to complete the sentences that explain why people think Dickens's books are funny.

comical	conversations	describes	humor	unusual

1. The characters are _____ and have _____ names.

2. Dickens _____ each character so well, you feel like you know them personally.

3. The _____ between the characters are often very funny.

4. Dickens helps us see _____ in the sad parts of life.

 SAY WHAT YOU THINK

Discuss the questions in a group.

1. Why do people think Charles Dickens's books are comical? Do you think this type of humor is funny?

2. Do you like to read comical books or novels? What kind of stories do you think are funny?

3. Who are famous funny people from your country? Why do you think they are popular?

Listening Skill | **Listening for specific information**

Listening for specific information means listening for the important details you need. We listen for specific information especially when we listen to news or weather reports, transportation schedules, and instructions.

Specific information includes details such as these.

- names of people or places
- numbers, dates, or times (See the Unit 3 Listening Skill, page 57.)
- events

 A. Read the information below. Then listen to Listening 1 again and write the missing information.

1. How many novels Charles Dickens wrote: _____

2. When Charles Dickens was born: _____

3. When his family moved to Kent in southeast England: _____

4. Where he got his first professional writing job:

   _____

5. How old he was when he stopped going to school: _____

B. Listen to the information about Charles Dickens. Write the missing information.

Tip for Success

Many radio stations put their radio shows on their websites. You can listen to them as many times as you like. This is a great way to practice listening.

Unlike some authors who only have one or two hits, _____ of

1

Dickens's 15 books became very famous. One of his most popular works

is *David Copperfield*. *David Copperfield* was Dickens's _____ novel,

2

which he wrote in _____. In the book, the main character, _____,

3   4

tells the story of his own life. Like Dickens, David has a difficult life when

he is young. His parents die when he is a boy, and he must go to work in a

_____. Many parts of the story are sad. But as always, the way Dickens

5

describes his characters makes readers laugh. In the end, David becomes a

successful _____, and lives a happy life. Late in his career, Dickens said

6

that David Copperfield was his favorite of all of the characters in his books.

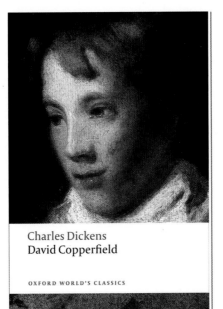

Charles Dickens
David Copperfield

OXFORD WORLD'S CLASSICS

 C. Go online for more practice with listening for specific information.

Before you speak in class, in a discussion, or for a presentation, it is useful to take time to gather some ideas about what you want to say. This will help you remember the vocabulary you need and share your ideas more clearly. A **word web** is a good way to gather your ideas.

Look at a student's word web for the question "What makes you laugh?"

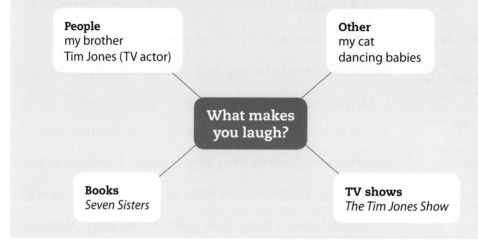

People
my brother
Tim Jones (TV actor)

Other
my cat
dancing babies

What makes you laugh?

Books
Seven Sisters

TV shows
The Tim Jones Show

A. Complete the word web below for the Unit Question, "Who makes you laugh?"

Who makes you laugh?

B. Compare word webs with a partner.

 **C.** Go online for more practice with making notes using a word web.

LISTENING 2 | What's Your Sense of Humor?

 UNIT OBJECTIVE You are going to listen to a guest speaker in a university lecture. In the lecture, he talks with the professor about people's sense of humor. As you listen to the lecture, gather information and ideas about who makes you laugh.

PREVIEW THE LISTENING

A. VOCABULARY Here are some words and phrases from Listening 2. Read the sentences. Circle the answer that best matches the meaning of each <u>underlined</u> word or phrase.

1. Sometimes it's difficult to <u>communicate</u> in another language.
   a. to talk to people   b. to look at people

2. Do you think it's funny to <u>make fun of</u> other people?
   a. to talk quietly to   b. to laugh at in an unkind way

3. Oh, no! I brought the <u>wrong</u> book to English class. This is my Spanish book.
   a. incorrect   b. interesting

Vocabulary Skill Review

In Unit 3, you learned about the suffixes *-ful* and *-ing*. Look at the word *interesting* in item 3. How can you change this word into a verb?

4. Some people don't like to show their <u>feelings</u>. They don't laugh or cry in front of other people.
   a. emotions such as happiness and anger   b. parts of the body

5. Sometimes I don't <u>understand</u> jokes in English. I feel confused about what is funny.
   a. to know what something means   b. to listen carefully to

6. Rei has a great sense of humor. She will <u>probably</u> laugh when I tell her the joke.
   a. not really   b. almost certainly

7. Marisol is <u>afraid</u> to stand in front of an audience. She feels very nervous.
   a. scared   b. happy

8. Close your eyes and <u>imagine</u> that you are at the beach.
   a. to make a picture in your mind   b. to draw a picture on paper

iQ ONLINE **B.** Go online for more practice with the vocabulary.

C. **PREVIEW** You are going to listen to a university lecture about different people's sense of humor. What is your sense of humor? Check (✓) the things that make you laugh. Then compare answers with your classmates.

☐ playing with babies / small children

☐ seeing cute animals

☐ other people falling down

☐ someone telling a joke

☐ watching comedy TV shows / cartoons

☐ reading humorous books

☐ making a mistake / doing something embarrassing

☐ other: _____

WORK WITH THE LISTENING

A. **LISTEN AND TAKE NOTES** Listen to the presentation and complete the student's word web with definitions of the four types of humor the presenter talks about.

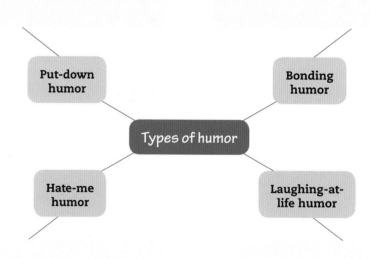

B. Compare word webs with a partner. Add one more box to each type of sense of humor in your word web. Then listen again and add one example for each sense of humor.

C. Read the items. Circle the answer that best describes each type of humor.

1. Put-down humor ___.
   a. helps us feel relaxed
   b. is the most common style
   c. makes fun of others

2. Bonding humor ___.
   a. is not very nice
   b. brings people together
   c. makes other people feel afraid

3. Hate-me humor makes fun of ___.
   a. people you dislike
   b. silly things
   c. yourself

4. Laughing-at-life humor ___.
   a. makes life easier
   b. is difficult to understand
   c. makes other people sad

D. Read the statements. Write *T* (true) or *F* (false). Then correct any false statements.

___ 1. Doctor Long feels that a sense of humor shows we are happy.

_____

___ 2. He thinks put-down humor is a way to make friends.

_____

___ 3. He says that people who use bonding humor like to tell jokes.

_____

___ 4. Hate-me humor does not mean we want people to dislike us.

_____

___ 5. Doctor Long says people who have the laughing-at-life humor style often have a sad life.

_____

E. Complete each sentence with your own words. Then compare answers with a partner.

1. Dr. Long says that humor helps us _____.

2. Humor is also one way that people _____.

3. Sometimes put-down humor can make people feel _____.

4. People who use bonding humor are _____

_____.

5. When people use hate-me humor, they _____.

6. People with the laughing-at-life humor style _____.

F. Read these examples of the four humor styles. Which styles are they? Write *put-down, bonding, hate-me,* or *laughing-at-life.*

_____ 1. A student often says he is not smart, is a bad student, etc., to make other students laugh at him.

_____ 2. A student gets a bad grade on a test. Another student says, "Congratulations! You got the lowest score!"

_____ 3. A student gets a bad grade on the test. She laughs and says, "I should study more next time."

_____ 4. A student likes to be in the center of a group, telling funny stories and jokes.

 G. Go online to listen to *Humor in Classic Literature* and check your comprehension.

 SAY WHAT YOU THINK

A. Discuss the questions in a group.

1. Do you agree that it's very important for a person to have a sense of humor? Why or why not?

2. Do you know any people with one of the four main humor types? Who are they? Describe them. What do they say or do?

3. Which style is most like your sense of humor? Why do you think so?

B. **Before you watch the video, discuss the questions in a group.**

When we communicate with other people, what are some examples of ways we show that we think something is funny . . .

- in person?
- in writing?
- on a computer or smartphone?

iQ ONLINE **C.** **Go online to watch the video about the science of smiling. Then check your comprehension.**

emotion *(n.)* a feeling
facial expression *(n.)* the way the face moves to show the way we feel
identify *(v.)* to understand
sophisticated *(adj.)* advanced and complicated

D. **Think about the unit video, Listening 1, and Listening 2 as you discuss the questions.**

1. Do you like to laugh at yourself? Why or why not?

2. How is humor different in different situations, for example, in person, on the phone, in writing, or on the computer?

Vocabulary Skill | Synonyms

Synonyms are words that have almost the same or a similar meaning. The dictionary often gives synonyms in the definition of a word. In the example, a synonym is given for *funny*.

---

fun·ny 🔑 /ˈfʌni/ *adjective* (fun·ni·er, fun·ni·est)
1 making you laugh or smile: *a funny story* ◆
He's so funny! ➔ **SYNONYM amusing**
2 strange or surprising: *There's a funny smell in this room.*

You can build your vocabulary by learning synonyms for words you already know. Learning synonyms will help you understand more when you listen.

All dictionary entries are from the *Oxford Basic American Dictionary for learners of English* © Oxford University Press 2011.

A. Read the sentences. Write a synonym from the box for each <u>underlined</u> word or phrase. You may use some synonyms more than once. Use your dictionary to help you.

famous	funny	huge	laugh	feelings

1. Did you read the book *James and the Giant Peach*? It's about an <u>enormous</u> peach.

   enormous: _____

2. My friend Tomás is <u>hilarious</u>. He always makes me laugh.

   hilarious: _____

3. Charles Dickens started writing when he was a young boy. But he didn't become <u>well known</u> until he published his first novel.

   well known: _____

4. Poets often write about different <u>emotions</u> such as anger or excitement.

   emotions: _____

5. Those two students are rude. They sit in the back of the class and <u>giggle</u>.

   giggle: _____

6. Children often make <u>silly</u> faces to make other kids laugh.

   silly: _____

B. Look in the dictionary to find one more synonym for each word. Write a sentence with each new synonym.

1. Word: huge   Synonym: _____

   Sentence: _____

2. Word: laugh   Synonym: _____

   Sentence: _____

3. Word: funny   Synonym: _____

   Sentence: _____

C. Read your synonyms and sentences from Activity B to a partner.

 **D.** Go online for more practice with synonyms.

SPEAKING

At the end of this unit, you are going to tell a joke or funny story to a group (or to the class). As you tell your joke or story, you will need to use appropriate eye contact, tone of voice, and pause.

Grammar | Simple present for informal narratives

When you tell a short, informal narrative, like a story or a joke, you can use the simple present even if the story happened in the past.

> A man **walks** into a shop and **sees** a little rabbit. He **asks** the shopkeeper, "Does your rabbit bite?"
> The shopkeeper **says**, "No, my rabbit doesn't bite."
> The man **touches** the rabbit, and the rabbit **bites** him.
> "Ouch!" he **says**. "You said your rabbit doesn't bite!"
> The shopkeeper **replies**, "That isn't my rabbit!"

A. Complete these jokes with the simple present form of the verbs in the box. Then listen and check your answers.

1.

bring	go	order	reply	say

A man and a woman _____ to a restaurant

for lunch. The woman _____ a bowl of soup.
                            2

A few minutes later, the waiter _____ the soup
                                       3

to the table. The man _____, "Excuse me. Your finger
                              4

is in my wife's soup." The waiter _____, "Oh, that's OK.
                                          5

It isn't too hot."

2.

answer	ask	be	say	think

A man _____ at the doctor's office.
              1

The doctor _____ him, "What's the trouble?"
                  2

The man _____, "I hurt everywhere. It hurts when
               3

I touch my head. It hurts when I touch my leg, and it hurts when

I touch my arm." The doctor _____ for a moment.
4

Then he _____, "I know what's wrong. Your finger
5

is broken!"

3.
| ask | look | say | see | stop | tell |

A man _____ his car at a traffic light.
1

A policeman stops next to him and _____ a penguin
2

in the car. The policeman _____ the man, "You can't
3

drive with a penguin in your car. Take that penguin to the zoo."

The man _____, "Yes, sir. I will." The next day, the
4

policeman sees the man's car again. The penguin is still in the car.

The policeman _____, "Why do you have that penguin?
5

I told you to take it to the zoo!" The man _____ at the
6

policeman and says, "I did that yesterday, and we had a great time!

Today we're going to the park!"

Critical Thinking (Tip)

In Activity B, you
learn a joke and
tell it. **Restating**, or
saying something
again in your own
words, is a good way
to share information.

B. Work in a group. Choose a joke from Activity A. Study the joke and
try to remember it. You can write some notes below to help you.
Take turns telling the jokes using the simple present. Look at your
classmates; don't read from your book.

_____

_____

_____

 C. Go online for more practice using the simple present for informal
narratives.

D. Go online for the grammar expansion.

The **simple present third-person singular** form of a regular verb ends in either -*s* or -*es*.

> He eat**s** a lot.
> She wash**es** her hands.

The pronunciation of this final sound depends on the sound at the end of the base verb. There are three possible sounds:

- The -*s* = /z/ when the sound is **voiced** (with sound). This includes all vowel sounds, and the consonants: /b/, /d/, /g/, /l/, /m/, /n/, /ŋ/ (ri**ng**), /r/, /ð/ (brea**th**, fa**th**er), and /v/.
- The -*s* = /s/ when the sound is **unvoiced** (without sound), including /f/, /k/, /p/, and /t/.
- The -*s*/-*es* = /əz/ when the final sound is an -*s* or -*z* like sound, including /dʒ/ (ju**dge**), /s/, /ʃ/ (wi**sh**), /tʃ/ (wat**ch**), and /z/.

Read and listen to the examples in the chart.

If the base verb ends in . . .	Base verb	*he / she / it*
a voiced sound, pronounce the third-person singular with /z/.	say tell give answer	say**s** tell**s** give**s** answer**s**
an unvoiced sound, pronounce the third-person singular with /s/.	laugh look stop eat	laugh**s** look**s** stop**s** eat**s**
an -*s* or -*z* like sound, pronounce the third-person singular with /əz/.	change miss wash watch	change**s** miss**es** wash**es** watch**es**

A. Read each joke and <u>underline</u> every simple present third-person verb ending in *-s* or *-es*. Write /z/, /s/, or /əz/ above each *-s* or *-es* to indicate the pronunciation.

1. **In the shop**

   A man walks into a shop and sees a little rabbit. He asks the

   shopkeeper, "Does your rabbit bite?"

   The shopkeeper says, "No, my rabbit doesn't bite."

   The man touches the rabbit, and the rabbit bites him.

   "Ouch!" he says. "You said your rabbit doesn't bite!"

   The shopkeeper replies, "That isn't my rabbit!"

Tip for Success

You can use the simple present third-person *-s* and *-es* pronunciation rules for the pronunciation of plural forms, too. For example, the plural of *boot* is *boots*. The *-s* is an unvoiced /s/ sound.

2. **At school**

   A five-year-old boy asks his teacher to help him put on his boots.

   The teacher says, "Of course," and he starts to help the boy. He pushes

   and pulls on the boots, but they don't go on the boy's feet. He gets very

   tired, so he takes a rest.

   The little boy says, "Teacher, these aren't my boots."

   "Why didn't you tell me?" the teacher asks.

   The boy replies, "They're my brother's boots. My mom made me wear

   them today."

   The teacher pushes and pulls on the boots some more, and finally,

   he gets them on the boy's feet.

   "OK! Now, where are your gloves?" he asks the boy.

   The boy answers, "I put them in my boots!"

B. Work with a partner. Take turns reading the jokes aloud. Use the correct pronunciation of the third-person singular endings.

iQ ONLINE **C.** Go online for more practice with simple present third-person *-s / -es*.

When you tell a story or a joke, there are different ways to make it more interesting.

- **Make eye contact with the listener(s).** This will help you connect with your audience and keep them interested.
- **Use your voice to express different feelings.** This helps the listener(s) understand the feelings of the people in the story.
- **Pause—stop speaking for a moment**—before you say the punch line (the end of a story or joke). This can help to make the ending a surprise.

Listen to the example.

> The man touches the rabbit, and the rabbit bites him.
> "Ouch!" he says. "You said your rabbit doesn't bite!"
> └──────┘   └────────────────────────────┘
> surprised/angry tone of voice
>
> The shopkeeper replies, "That isn't my rabbit!"
>   ↑
>   pause

A. Listen to the joke. <u>Underline</u> the places where the speaker uses tone of voice. Draw an arrow (↑) where the speaker pauses.

A man is at the doctor's office. The doctor asks him, "What's the trouble?" The man answers, "I hurt everywhere. It hurts when I touch my head. It hurts when I touch my leg, and it hurts when I touch my arm." The doctor thinks for a moment. Then he says, "I know what's wrong. Your finger is broken!"

B. Work with a partner. Read the joke in Activity A aloud. Practice making eye contact, using tone of voice, and pausing.

C. Read these excerpts from jokes. <u>Underline</u> the places where you can use tone of voice. Draw an arrow (↑) where you can pause.

1. A few minutes later, the waiter brings the soup to the table. The man says, "Excuse me. Your finger is in my wife's soup." The waiter replies, "Oh, that's OK. It isn't too hot."

2. The next day, the policeman sees the man's car again. The penguin is still in the car. The policeman asks, "Why do you have that penguin? I told you to take it to the zoo!" The man looks at the policeman and says, "I did that yesterday, and we had a great time! Today we're going to the park!"

D. Work in a group. Take turns reading aloud the excerpts in Activity C. Remember to make eye contact, use tone of voice, and pause before the end.

E. Go online for more practice with using eye contact, tone of voice, and pause.

Unit Assignment	Tell a joke or a funny story

In this assignment, you are going to tell a joke or funny story to a group (or to the class). As you prepare your joke or story, think about the Unit Question, "Who makes you laugh?" Use information from Listening 1, Listening 2, the unit video, and your work in the unit to support your joke or story. Refer to the Self-Assessment checklist on page 96.

CONSIDER THE IDEAS

A. Read the joke and try to guess the punch line (the last line).

A tourist visits Sydney, Australia. He wants to go to the beach. But he doesn't know how to get there. He sees a policeman. He waves to the policeman and says, "Excuse me! Can you help me?"

The policeman comes over and says, "Yes, sir. How can I help you?"

The tourist says, "Can you tell me the fastest way to get to the beach?"

The policeman asks, "Are you walking or driving?"

The tourist answers, "Driving."

The policeman answers, "_____."

B. Listen to an Australian comedian tell the joke in Activity A. Write the punch line in Activity A above.

C. Listen again and discuss these questions with a partner.

1. Do you understand the joke?

2. Do you think the comedian was good? Why or why not?

3. Where in the joke did the comedian use tone of voice or pause? Underline where his tone of voice changed and draw an arrow (↑) where there was a pause.

PREPARE AND SPEAK

A. GATHER IDEAS Think of a joke or a funny story you want to tell. It can be a joke or story you know or a story about something that happened to you or someone you know. Use a word web to make notes and gather ideas for your joke or story.

B. ORGANIZE IDEAS Make notes about your joke or story. Remember that you can use the simple present. Then complete the tasks below.

1. Underline places in your joke or story where you can use tone of voice. Draw an arrow (↑) in the place where you can pause (before the punch line).

2. Practice telling your joke or funny story to a partner. Use eye contact, tone of voice, and a pause to make the joke more interesting.

C. SPEAK Tell your joke or story to a group (or to the class). Refer to the Self-Assessment checklist on page 96 before you begin.

iQ ONLINE Go online for your alternate Unit Assignment.

CHECK AND REFLECT

A. CHECK **Think about the Unit Assignment as you complete the Self-Assessment checklist.**

Yes	No	SELF-ASSESSMENT
☐	☐	I was able to speak easily about the topic.
☐	☐	I used a word web to gather ideas and take notes.
☐	☐	My partner/group/class understood me and thought I was funny.
☐	☐	I used the simple present to tell a joke/funny story.
☐	☐	I used vocabulary from the unit.
☐	☐	I used eye contact, tone of voice, and pause when telling a joke/funny story.
☐	☐	I pronounced the simple present third-person -s/-es correctly.

iQ ONLINE **B.** REFLECT **Go to the Online Discussion Board to discuss these questions.**

1. What is something new you learned in this unit?

2. Look back at the Unit Question—Who makes you laugh? Is your answer different now than when you started the unit? If yes, how is it different? Why?

TRACK YOUR SUCCESS

Circle the words and phrases you have learned in this unit.

Nouns
feelings 🔑
hit 🔑

Verbs
communicate 🔑 `AWL`
describe 🔑
imagine 🔑
understand 🔑

Adjectives
afraid 🔑
comical
funny 🔑
huge 🔑
professional 🔑 `AWL`
talented
wrong 🔑

Adverbs
however 🔑
probably 🔑

Phrases
make fun of
sense of humor

🔑 Oxford 2000 keywords
`AWL` Academic Word List

Check (✓) the skills you learned. If you need more work on a skill, refer to the page(s) in parentheses.

LISTENING ☐	I can listen for specific information. (p. 80)
NOTE TAKING ☐	I can use a word web to make notes and gather ideas. (p. 82)
VOCABULARY ☐	I can recognize and use synonyms. (p. 87)
GRAMMAR ☐	I can recognize and use the simple present for informal narratives. (p. 89)
PRONUNCIATION ☐	I can recognize and pronounce the simple present third-person -s/-es. (p. 91)
SPEAKING ☐	I can use eye contact, tone of voice, and pause. (p. 93)
UNIT OBJECTIVE ▶▶▶▶ ☐	I can gather information and ideas to tell a joke or a funny story.

UNIT **5**

Psychology

NOTE TAKING ▶	using numbered lists to organize information
LISTENING ▶	listening for signal words and phrases
VOCABULARY ▶	using the dictionary
GRAMMAR ▶	gerunds as subjects or objects
PRONUNCIATION ▶	intonation in questions
SPEAKING ▶	asking for and giving opinions

UNIT QUESTION

Why do we enjoy sports?

A Discuss these questions with your classmates.

1. What sports do you like to play? Are there some sports you like to watch?

2. What sports are popular in your country?

3. Look at the picture. What sport are these people playing? Is it popular in your country?

UNIT
OBJECTIVE ▶▶▶▶ Listen to a lecture and a conversation. Gather
information and ideas to participate in a group
interview about sports preferences.

B Listen to *The Q Classroom* online. Then write the reasons
why the students enjoy each sport.

> a. I can express myself when I play.
>
> b. It helps me relax at the end of the day.
>
> c. ~~It's good to play on a team.~~
>
> d. It's a part of my family life.
>
> e. I can study better.

	Sports	Reasons
Felix	soccer	1. _c. It's good to play on a team._
	tennis	2. _____
Yuna	volleyball	3. _____
	basketball	4. _____
Marcus	soccer	5. _____

C Go to the Online Discussion Board to discuss the Unit Question with
your classmates.

D Match the pictures with the sports.

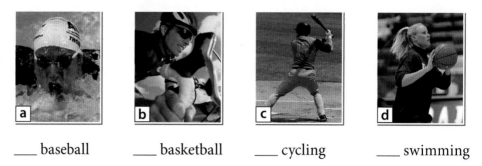

___ baseball ___ basketball ___ cycling ___ swimming

E Walk around and ask your classmates questions. Try to find a different classmate for each activity in the chart. Ask a follow-up question to get more information.

A: *Excuse me. Do you play on a sports team?*
B: *Yes, I do.*
A: *Great! What sport do you play?*

Find a classmate who . . .	Classmate's name	More information
1. plays on a sports team.		
2. likes swimming.		
3. enjoys watching sports on TV.		
4. plays tennis well.		
5. likes the same sports team as you.		
6. likes to run.		

F What did you learn about your classmates? Share two things with the class.

Use **numbered lists** as a way to organize information in your notes. This is especially useful when a speaker lists a number of items within a topic. For example, a speaker may name different ways that exercise is good for us, or reasons why it's important for children to get exercise.

Often, the speaker will use signal words and phrases, such as *first of all*, *secondly*, or *another*. Signal words and phrases can help you identify new items in a list.

Listen to the beginning of a lecture about ways that exercise is good for older people. Then read a student's notes.

---

1. *helps bodies stay healthy*
   - *get sick less*
   - *fewer physical pains*
   - *injured less*
2. *increases strength, balance*
   - *helps keep muscles strong, so can still do what they need to do*
   - *helps avoid accidents, like falling*

A. Listen to the rest of the lecture. Take notes on the additional reasons the speaker gives. Remember to continue the student's numbered list above.

B. Compare notes with a partner.

iQ ONLINE **C.** Go online for more practice with using numbered lists to organize information.

LISTENING 1 | Body and Mind

 You are going to listen to a scientist giving a university lecture about the effects of doing sports and why exercise is good for people. As you listen to the lecture, gather information and ideas about why we enjoy sports.

PREVIEW THE LISTENING

A. **VOCABULARY** Here are some words and phrases from Listening 1. Read the sentences. Then write each <u>underlined</u> word or phrase next to the correct definition.

1. One <u>benefit</u> of doing sports is that it can give you more energy.

2. All <u>humans</u> need exercise to stay healthy.

3. Steve is very <u>active</u>. He plays soccer and baseball, and he enjoys cycling, too.

4. Even a little exercise every day can <u>improve</u> your health.

5. When we exercise, it helps to "wake up" our <u>brain</u>.

6. I'm worried about my baseball game after school today. I can't <u>concentrate</u> on my school work!

7. To be a good soccer player, you need a lot of <u>skill</u>.

8. Playing sports is very good for you. It can <u>lower stress</u> and help you feel calm.

a. _____ (*phrasal verb*) to make you feel more relaxed

b. _____ (*verb*) to give all your attention to something

c. _____ (*noun*) something that is good or helpful

d. _____ (*noun*) the part inside a person's head that thinks and feels

e. _____ (*noun*) the ability to do something well

f. _____ (*adjective*) always busy; doing many things

g. _____ (*verb*) to make something better

h. _____ (*noun*) people

 **B.** Go online for more practice with the vocabulary.

C. PREVIEW You are going to listen to a scientist giving a university lecture about the effects of doing sports and why exercise is good for people.

Check (✓) the ways you think doing sports and exercise helps people.

☐ concentration   ☐ friendship   ☐ learning

☐ family connections   ☐ health   ☐ stress

WORK WITH THE LISTENING

A. LISTEN AND TAKE NOTES Listen to the lecture and identify the six ways that sports benefit the human mind. On a separate sheet of paper, list the six benefits in a numbered list to organize the information. Leave space between them so you can add details later.

B. Compare lists with a partner. Discuss any details you remember about each benefit.

C. Listen again and add details under each numbered benefit on your list.

D. Match the two halves of the main ideas from the listening.

_____ 1. Even in ancient times,   a. we feel better and live longer.

_____ 2. Playing sports helps memory, so   b. they feel like part of a family.

_____ 3. When our bodies work hard,   c. can teach us important life skills.

_____ 4. Joining a sports team   d. it is especially good for students.

_____ 5. Just watching sports   e. can help people feel better.

_____ 6. When people have a favorite sports team,   f. humans enjoyed playing and watching sports.

E. Read the questions. Circle the correct answer.

1. When did humans begin playing and watching sports?
   a. Over 400 years ago.
   b. Over 4,000 years ago.
   c. Over 4,000,000 years ago.

2. What type of sports are especially good for our health?
   a. Sports that began in China.
   b. Sports that we do on a team.
   c. Sports that require a lot of running.

3. What did the study show about children who do sports?
   a. Their brains are huge.
   b. They use their brains more.
   c. They do better in school.

4. What does the scientist say are "important skills for life"?
   a. Bringing people together and making friends.
   b. Being part of a team and working together.
   c. Going to school and working hard.

5. How do some people feel when they have a favorite sports team?
   a. They feel like they are part of a group.
   b. They feel like they want to do the sport.
   c. They feel like they want to watch TV.

F. **Read the statements. Write *T* (true) or *F* (false). Write information from the lecture to explain your answers.**

____ 1. Some sports played today are very old.

_____

____ 2. Walking is better for our health than running.

_____

____ 3. Exercise makes our bodies and brains tired.

_____

____ 4. People who play sports may be more successful in life.

_____

____ 5. It is dangerous for people with stress to watch sports on TV.

_____

SAY WHAT YOU THINK

Discuss the questions in a group.

1. Think about the lecture. What benefits do sports and exercise have on the body? What benefits do they have on the mind?

2. Do sports and exercise have any of these benefits in your life? Which ones?

3. What is one interesting thing you learned from the lecture?

| Listening Skill | Listening for signal words and phrases |

In a lecture, speakers use special words and phrases to **signal** when they introduce a new topic. These words and phrases help you follow a lecture better.

You will hear different words and phrases in different parts of the lecture.

At the beginning:	**First**, let's think about how sports are important. . . .
	The first important benefit of doing sports **is that** it helps us stay healthy.
In the middle:	**The next thing I'll talk about** is the history of sports.
	In addition, watching sports can be good for us.
	Also, it's fun and relaxing.
At the end:	**The last/final topic** is how sports bring people together.
	Finally, when people have a favorite sports team, they feel like they are part of a group.

Tip for Success

When you take notes, it's helpful to listen for words and phrases such as *first*, *the second*, *one more*, and *in addition*. These words and phrases can help you organize the speaker's main points.

A. Listen to these excerpts from Listening 1. Complete the sentences with the words and phrases you hear.

1. _____ of doing sports is that it helps us stay healthy. It's important for us to be active.

2. _____ important thing that sports do is bring people together. Playing a sport is a great way to make friends.

3. _____, watching sports can be good for us, too. Many people enjoy watching their favorite team play a soccer or baseball game on TV, or even going to see a live game.

4. _____, when people have a favorite sports team, they feel like they are part of a group—almost like a family. It's a good feeling.

B. Work with a partner. Take turns reading your completed sentences from Activity A. Discuss any differences in your answers.

 C. Go online for more practice with listening for signal words and phrases.

LISTENING 2 | Sports in Our Lives

 You are going to listen to four people talk about the importance of sports in their lives. As you listen to the conversation, gather information and ideas about why we enjoy sports.

PREVIEW THE LISTENING

Vocabulary Skill Review

In Unit 4, you learned that synonyms are words that have almost the same or similar meaning. Can you find a synonym for the word *protect*?

A. **VOCABULARY** Here are some words from Listening 2. Read their definitions. Then complete each sentence below with the correct word.

> **coach** (*noun*) a sports trainer or instructor
> **escape** (*verb*) 🔑 to get free from someone or something
> **exciting** (*adjective*) 🔑 fun; causing you to feel a lot of energy
> **forget** (*verb*) 🔑 to stop thinking about something; to not remember
> **patient** (*adjective*) 🔑 able to stay calm when you are waiting or when you have problems
> **protect** (*verb*) 🔑 to keep safe
> **traditional** (*adjective*) old; from a long time ago

🔑 Oxford 2000 keywords

1. When I have a lot of stress and I need to _____ from my problems, I go on a long run.

2. Our basketball team has an excellent _____. He teaches us a lot of great skills.

3. Karate is a(n) _____ sport. It started many years ago in Japan.

4. I think basketball is the most _____ sport to watch. The players have to be very fast.

5. I didn't see you at soccer practice today. Did you _____?

6. You need to be _____ when you are learning a sport. It takes time to learn a new skill.

7. You should wear a helmet when you ride a bike. It will _____ your head if you fall.

B. Go online for more practice with the vocabulary.

C. **PREVIEW** You are going to listen to four people talk about the importance of sports in their lives. Match each statement from the listening with a photo.

a. Our coach, Mr. Wells, teaches us a lot of new skills.
b. Sometimes I go swimming or running, but I enjoy cycling the most.
c. In Canada, where I'm from, ice hockey is the most popular sport.
d. For example, judo and karate are famous sports that came from Japan.

Marco ____   Eric ____   Takumi ____   Alex ____

WORK WITH THE LISTENING

A. **LISTEN AND TAKE NOTES** Listen to the four people. On a separate sheet of paper, take notes on the reasons they say they enjoy sports. Use a numbered list to organize the information.

B. Compare notes with a partner. Discuss any differences in your notes.

C. Read the information below. Which person is each fact about? Listen again and match the person with the information.

____ 1. Marco   a. can use the sport as transportation

____   b. does not play on a team

____ 2. Eric   c. has a favorite hometown team

____   d. learns skills for dangerous situations

____ 3. Takumi   e. describes a traditional national sport

____   f. practices the sport every day

____ 4. Alex   g. recently joined a sports team

____   h. watches the sport, but may not play it

D. Compare answers with a partner. Explain how you got your answers using information and examples from the listening.

E. Read the questions. Then write answers in complete sentences.

1. When did Marco join the soccer team?

_____

2. When and for how long does Marco's team practice?

_____

3. Why does Eric like hockey?

_____

4. Who does Eric watch hockey games with?

_____

5. What sports does Takumi say are the most popular in Japan?

_____

6. What do judo and karate players have to learn?

_____

7. How often does Alex exercise?

_____

8. What sports does Alex enjoy?

_____

iQ ONLINE **F.** Go online to listen to *Nikolai Andrianov* and check your comprehension.

SAY WHAT YOU THINK

A. Discuss the questions in a group.

1. Do you share the speakers' feelings about sports?

2. Which person are you most similar to? Why?

3. In what ways are sports important in your life?

B. Before you watch the video, discuss the questions in a group.

1. What are popular sports for young children in your country?

2. At what age do children usually start playing competitive sports?

iQ ONLINE **C.** Go online to watch the video about when children should get involved in sports. Then check your comprehension.

> **VIDEO VOCABULARY**
>
> **emotionally** *(adv.)* relating to feelings
> **physically** *(adv.)* relating to the body
> **push someone to do something** *(phr. v.)* to pressure; to encourage too strongly
> **terrific** *(adj.)* excellent

D. Think about the unit video, Listening 1, and Listening 2 as you discuss the questions.

1. How are sports different now from in the past? Are any traditional sports still popular in your country? What are some new sports?

2. Are there any sports or athletes that make you feel proud of your country? Why?

3. At what age do children usually get involved in sports in your country? Is there a lot of pressure for kids to be successful at sports?

The dictionary gives more than one **definition** for many words. Be sure to choose the definition that best fits the context in which you found the word.

For example, the word *benefit* has two meanings in the dictionary.

> **ben·e·fit¹** 🔑 **AWL** /ˈbɛnəfɪt/ *noun*
> **1** [*count*] something that is good or helpful:
> *What are the **benefits of** having a computer? ♦ I did it **for** your **benefit** (= to help you).*
> **2** [*count, noncount*] (**POLITICS**, **BUSINESS**) money or other advantages that you get from your job, the government, or a company you belong to:
> *unemployment benefits ♦ All our employees receive medical benefits in addition to their salary.*

You want the definition as used in this sentence.

> The first important **benefit** of doing sports is that it helps us stay healthy.

You can see that definition 1 is correct for this use of the word *benefit*.

All dictionary entries are from the *Oxford Basic American Dictionary for learners of English* © Oxford University Press 2011.

Critical Thinking **Tip**

In Activity A, you have to **determine** which definition is the best. You use the context to choose between the different meanings. Using context to determine meaning is one way to improve your vocabulary skills.

A. Read the sentences and the dictionary definitions. Write the number of the correct definition of each <u>underlined</u> word.

_____ 1. The first important benefit of doing sports is that it helps us stay healthy. It's important for us to be <u>active</u>.

> **ac·tive** 🔑 /ˈæktɪv/ *adjective*
> **1** If you are **active**, you are always busy and able to do a lot of things: *My grandmother is 75 but she's still very active.*
> **2** (**ENGLISH LANGUAGE ARTS**) (used about a verb or sentence) when the person or thing doing the action is the subject of the verb ↪ **ANTONYM passive**

_____ 2. Hockey is <u>special</u> to me because it brings my family together and makes us closer.

> **spe·cial¹** 🔑 /ˈspɛʃl/ *adjective*
> **1** not usual or ordinary; important for a reason: *I got a new job, so we're having a special dinner.*
> **2** for a particular person or thing: *He goes to a special school for deaf children.*

____ 3. When we play sports, especially when we do a lot of running, our heart goes faster and <u>moves</u> blood to the different parts of our bodies.

> **move¹** 🔑 /muv/ *verb* (moves, mov·ing, moved)
> **1** to go from one place to another; to change the way you are standing or sitting: *Don't get off the bus while it's moving.* ◆ *We **moved to** the front of the queue.*
> **2** to put something in another place or another way: *Can you move your car, please?*
> **3** to go to live in another place: *They sold their house in Detroit and **moved to** Ann Arbor.*
> **4** to cause someone to have strong feelings, especially of sadness: *The news report **moved** me to tears.*

____ 4. We can concentrate and learn better. For example, my <u>study</u> showed that children who do some kind of sports usually do better in school.

> **stud·y²** 🔑 /'stʌdi/ *noun* (plural stud·ies)
> **1** [*noncount*] the activity of learning about something: *Biology is **the study of** living things.*
> **2 studies** [*plural*] the subjects that you study: *He's taking a class in **business studies**.*
> **3** [*count*] a room in a house where you go to study, read, or write
> **4** [*count*] a piece of research that is done to learn more about a question or subject: *They are doing a study of the causes of heart disease.*

____ 5. Riding my bike gives me a way to forget about my <u>problems</u>.

> **prob·lem** 🔑 /'prɑbləm/ *noun* [*count*]
> **1** something that is difficult; something that makes you worry: *She has a lot of problems. Her husband is sick and she may lose her job.* ◆ *There is a problem with my phone – it doesn't work.*
> **2** a question that you must answer by thinking about it: *I can't **solve** this **problem**.*
> **no problem** (*informal*) words you use to say that something is easy and you don't mind doing it: *"Can you fix this?" "Sure, no problem."*

B. Compare answers with a partner.

 C. Go online for more practice with using the dictionary.

SPEAKING

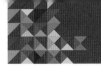

 At the end of this unit, you are going to interview a group of classmates about their sports preferences. As you speak, you will need to ask for and give opinions.

Grammar   Gerunds as subjects or objects

A **gerund** is an *-ing* form of a verb that can take the place of a noun or pronoun. Because gerunds end in *-ing*, they may <u>look</u> like verbs, but they are <u>not</u> verbs. A gerund acts as a noun.

- Gerunds are often the **subject** of a sentence. Several verbs that express actions or states are commonly gerunds.

  Joining a sports team is a good way to make friends.
  Being part of a team can teach us important skills.

- Gerunds can also be the **object** (a noun or noun phrase that follows a verb) of a sentence. Many common verbs are followed by gerunds, such as *avoid, discuss, dislike, enjoy, hate, like, love,* and *prefer.*

  I <u>like</u> **playing** soccer with my friends.
  My sister <u>enjoys</u> **swimming** in the summer.
  Do you <u>prefer</u> **exercising** in a gym?
  I <u>hate</u> **running** long distances.

 A. Read the excerpts from Listening 2. Guess the missing gerunds. Then listen and complete the excerpts with the correct gerunds.

1. This year, I joined the soccer team at my high school. _____ on a team is so much fun. The other players are great. I've made a lot of new friends already.

2. Our coach, Mr. Wells, teaches us a lot of new skills. We practice every day after school for two hours. _____ my skills makes me feel good about myself.

3. I like hockey because it's a fast, exciting game. I love _____ the players fly down the ice. Everyone in my family likes the Jets. That's the hockey team from my hometown. When they play, my brother, my father, and I enjoy _____ the games on TV.

4. These days, baseball and soccer are the most popular sports in Japan, but we have many traditional sports, too. For example, judo and karate are famous sports that came from Japan. _____ these sports takes a long time, and players practice many hours and work very hard.

5. I can't imagine my life without sports. _____ healthy is important to me. I don't play on any sports teams. I prefer _____ by myself. I do some kind of exercise every day. Sometimes I go swimming or running, but I enjoy _____ the most.

B. Write five sentences about how sports are important in your life. Use a gerund as a subject or object. Use a different verb for each sentence.

be	exercise	join	play	watch

1. _____

2. _____

3. _____

4. _____

5. _____

C. Read your sentences to a partner.

D. Go online for more practice with gerunds as subjects or objects.

E. Go online for the grammar expansion.

Yes/No **questions** ask for an answer of yes or no. *Yes/No* questions have rising intonation at the end.

Listen and repeat these examples.

Do you exercise every day?

Do you and your family watch a lot of sports on TV?

Are you going to the soccer game this weekend?

Information questions ask for information about *who, what, why, when, where, how,* or *how often.* Information questions have falling intonation at the end.

Listen and repeat these examples.

When did you start playing baseball?

Who is your favorite basketball team?

How often do you go to a live sports game?

Questions of choice ask a person to choose between two things. Questions of choice have rising-falling intonation at the end.

Listen and repeat these examples.

Which do you like better, soccer or baseball?

Do you usually exercise alone or with friends?

Do you prefer playing sports or watching sports?

A. Read the questions. What type of question is each one?
Write *Y/N* (yes/no), *I* (information), or *C* (choice).

____ 1. Are you better at playing tennis or baseball?

____ 2. Who is your favorite athlete?

____ 3. What is an example of a traditional sport from your country?

____ 4. Is your favorite athlete from your country or another country?

____ 5. Do you exercise outside, or do you go to the gym?

____ 6. Do you enjoy watching sports on TV?

____ 7. What kind of sports do you like better, winter sports or summer sports?

B. Look again at Activity A on page 114. For each question, draw arrows like the ones in the examples in the skill box to show the correct intonation. Then listen and repeat each question.

iQ ONLINE **C.** Go online for more practice with intonation in questions.

Speaking Skill Asking for and giving opinions

At school, at work, and in our daily lives, we often ask for and give **opinions**. Knowing common phrases can help you understand more easily and speak more naturally.

Asking for opinions

Use these phrases when you want to know someone's opinion.

What do you think of the Jets' new player?
How do you feel about traditional sports?
Do you think they will win the game?
I think Marco is the best player on the team. **Don't you agree?**

Giving your opinion

Use these phrases when you want to give your opinion.

I think exercising in a gym is boring.
I don't think this team is very good.
I feel that more young people should join sports teams.
In my opinion, the Red Sox are the best baseball team.

A. Read the topics in the box. Choose three topics and write a question for each. Use phrases from the Speaking Skill box above.

traditional sports	the best soccer team from your country
gyms	the best athlete from your country
children and sports	watching sports on TV

1. _____ ?

2. _____ ?

3. _____ ?

B. Work with a partner. Take turns asking and answering the questions in Activity A.

 C. Go online for more practice with asking for and giving opinions.

UNIT OBJECTIVE ▶▶▶▶ In this assignment, you are going to interview your classmates about their sports preferences and answer questions about your own. As you prepare your interview questions and answers, think about the Unit Question, "Why do we enjoy sports?" Use information from Listening 1, Listening 2, the unit video, and your work in the unit to support your interviews. Refer to the Self-Assessment checklist on page 118.

CONSIDER THE IDEAS

Read the questions. Then listen to an interview with a Qatari university student about his sports preferences. Check (✓) the questions you hear.

☐ 1. What kinds of sports do you like to do?

☐ 2. What do you think of our university soccer team?

☐ 3. Why do you like volleyball?

☐ 4. Do you prefer soccer or volleyball?

☐ 5. Which do you like better, indoor volleyball or beach volleyball?

☐ 6. Who are your favorite volleyball players?

PREPARE AND SPEAK

A. GATHER IDEAS Work in a group. Read the topics below. Brainstorm a list of questions you can ask to find out about your classmates' sports preferences.

- their opinions about different types of sports
- ways sports and exercise are important in their lives
- teams or players they like or dislike
- sports from different cultures
- traditional sports

B. ORGANIZE IDEAS As a group, choose five questions from your list to ask your classmates. Make a T-chart like the one below. Write only the questions in the T-chart now. You will complete the Answers column when you interview your classmates.

Questions	Answers

C. SPEAK Follow these steps. Refer to the Self-Assessment checklist on page 118 before you begin.

1. Join your group with another group. Group A takes turns asking Group B questions. Write each member's answers in the T-chart. Then Group B interviews Group A.

2. Look at the answers in your T-chart. What sports, teams, or athletes are the most popular? The least popular? How are sports and exercise important in your classmates' lives? Tell the class.

iQ ONLINE **D.** Go online for your alternate Unit Assignment.

CHECK AND REFLECT

A. CHECK Think about the Unit Assignment as you complete the Self-Assessment checklist.

SELF-ASSESSMENT		
Yes	No	
☐	☐	I was able to speak easily about the topic.
☐	☐	I used a numbered list to organize information.
☐	☐	My partner/group/class understood me.
☐	☐	I used gerunds as subjects or objects.
☐	☐	I used vocabulary from the unit.
☐	☐	I asked for and gave opinions.
☐	☐	I used correct intonation in questions.

iQ ONLINE **B. REFLECT** Go to the Online Discussion Board to discuss these questions.

1. What is something new you learned in this unit?

2. Look back at the Unit Question—Why do we enjoy sports? Is your answer different now than when you started the unit? If yes, how is it different? Why?

TRACK YOUR SUCCESS

Circle the words and phrases you have learned in this unit.

Nouns
benefit 🔑 AWL
brain 🔑
coach
human 🔑
problem 🔑
skill 🔑
study 🔑

Verbs
concentrate 🔑 AWL
escape 🔑
forget 🔑
improve 🔑
move 🔑
protect 🔑

Phrasal Verb
lower stress

Adjectives
active 🔑
exciting 🔑
patient 🔑
special 🔑
traditional AWL

Phrases
Also, . . .
Do you think . . . ?
Don't you agree?
Finally, . . .
First, . . .

How do you feel
  about . . . ?
I think . . .
I don't think . . .
I feel that . . .
In addition, . . .
In my opinion, . . .
The first important . . .
The next thing I'll talk
  about is . . .
The last/final topic . . .
What do you think
  of . . . ?

🔑 Oxford 2000 keywords
AWL Academic Word List

Check (✓) the skills you learned. If you need more work on a skill, refer to the page(s) in parentheses.

NOTE TAKING ☐	I can use numbered lists to organize information. (p. 101)
LISTENING ☐	I can listen for signal words and phrases. (p. 105)
VOCABULARY ☐	I can choose the correct dictionary definition. (p. 110)
GRAMMAR ☐	I can use and recognize gerunds as subjects or objects. (p. 112)
PRONUNCIATION ☐	I can use correct intonation in questions. (p. 114)
SPEAKING ☐	I can ask for and give opinions. (p. 115)
UNIT OBJECTIVE ▶▶▶ ☐	I can gather information and ideas to participate in a group interview about sports preferences.

<table>
<tr><td rowspan="6">UNIT 6
Philosophy</td><td>NOTE TAKING ▶</td><td>using abbreviations and symbols</td></tr>
</table>

NOTE TAKING ▶	using abbreviations and symbols
LISTENING ▶	making inferences
VOCABULARY ▶	percentages and fractions
GRAMMAR ▶	conjunctions *and* and *but*
PRONUNCIATION ▶	linking consonants to vowels
SPEAKING ▶	sourcing information

UNIT QUESTION

When is honesty important?

A Discuss these questions with your classmates.

1. What are some examples of honest things that people do?

2. What are some examples of dishonest things that people do?

3. Look at the photo. Where are these people? What is happening? Why is it important for people to be honest here?

B Listen to *The Q Classroom* online. Then answer these questions.

1. In what situations do the students think it's important to be honest?

2. What examples do they give of situations when honesty can be negative?

3. Do you think it is OK to be dishonest sometimes? When?

iQ ONLINE **C** Go to the Online Discussion Board to discuss the Unit Question with your classmates.

UNIT
OBJECTIVE  Listen to a TV news report and two conversations.
Gather information and ideas to conduct a survey
on honesty and dishonesty. Then report your results
to the class.

D Look at the survey below. How wrong are these actions? Check (✓) your opinion.

Are you honest?

Complete the survey to see how honest you are!

	Not Wrong	A little wrong	Very wrong
1. Saying you are younger or older than you really are	○	○	○
2. Borrowing something from a friend or family member without asking	○	○	○
3. Sharing quiz or test answers with a classmate	○	○	○
4. Parking in a no-parking zone	○	○	○
5. Finding money on the street and keeping it	○	○	○
6. Copying a school report from the Internet	○	○	○
7. Going in front of a long line of people without waiting	○	○	○
8. Telling an employer you have more work experience than you really do	○	○	○

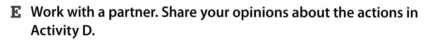

Results

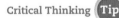
Critical Thinking **Tip**

In Activity D, you have to **judge** an action. **Judging** right or wrong is an important critical thinking skill, and it helps you share your opinions in Activity E.

E Work with a partner. Share your opinions about the actions in Activity D.

A: I think <u>saying you are younger or older than you really are</u> is very wrong.

B: I think it's only a little wrong.

When you take notes, you need to write a lot of information quickly. Using **abbreviations** (short forms of longer words) and symbols can save time and help you take notes more quickly, so you don't miss important information.

There are two common ways to abbreviate longer words in English.

- Write the first few letters of the word.

ex	example	org	organization	uni	university
imp	important	prob	problem	tech	technology
info	information				

- Leave out all or most vowels in the word.

dept	department	govt	government
dvlp	develop	mgr	manager

There are some common letter abbreviations and symbols used to stand for English words. Here are some common abbreviations used in English.

b/c	because	incl.	including	w/	with
co.	company	no.	number	w/o	without
etc.	et cetera (and so on)				

Here are some symbols used in English.

+ / &	and	>	more than
=	equal to / the same as	#	number
<	less than	%	percent

Listen to the beginning of a report about dishonesty and résumés. Look at the student's notes and notice the use of abbreviations and symbols.

> *res – 1 of mst common ways people are dshnst*
>
> *study by bus mgmt. org – 53% res incl. false info*
>
> *exs of dshnsty – chnging dates to make past*
> *emplmnt lnger, false grad dates to appr yngr*

A. Listen to the rest of the report. On a separate sheet of paper, take notes. Use abbreviations and symbols to save time.

B. Compare notes with a partner.

 C. Go online for more practice with using abbreviations and symbols.

LISTENING

LISTENING 1 | Dishonesty in Schools

UNIT OBJECTIVE You are going to listen to a TV news report about cheating in schools. As you listen to the news report, gather information and ideas about when honesty is important.

PREVIEW THE LISTENING

A. **VOCABULARY** Here are some words and phrases from Listening 1. Read the sentences. Then write each <u>underlined</u> word or phrase next to the correct definition.

1. He didn't study, but he got an A on the test. Did he <u>cheat</u>?

2. The teacher took a <u>survey</u> to find out how many students use the Internet. All of the students answered yes.

3. <u>According to</u> a magazine article, most people tell lies sometimes.

4. Recent <u>technology</u>, such as the Internet and cell phones, makes communication fast and easy.

5. About a <u>quarter</u> of the class are international students.

6. I want to get a good <u>grade</u> on my final exam in math.

7. I feel sad when I hear stories about children who don't have enough food. I think it's wrong for children to <u>suffer</u>.

a. _____ (*noun*) the number or letter that shows how well you have done in school

b. _____ (*verb*) to do something that is not honest or fair

c. _____ (*noun*) questions to find out what people think or do

d. _____ (*noun*) knowledge about science and about how things work

e. _____ (*noun*) 25 percent

f. _____ (*verb*) to feel pain, sadness, or another unpleasant feeling

g. _____ (*phrase*) as something or someone says

Oxford 2000 keywords

B. Go online for more practice with the vocabulary.

C. **PREVIEW** You are going to listen to a TV news report about cheating in schools.

What percentage of U.S. high school students do you think say they cheat?

☐ 25 percent ☐ 50 percent ☐ 75 percent

WORK WITH THE LISTENING

A. **LISTEN AND TAKE NOTES** Read these questions. Then listen to the news report and take notes on the answers. Use abbreviations and symbols when possible.

1. What did a recent survey find? What examples does the report give of ways students cheat?

   _____

   _____

   _____

2. Why does teacher Wendy Smith think students are cheating more?

   _____

   _____

   _____

3. What does teacher Don Quinn think about students using the Internet for research?

   _____

   _____

   _____

4. What examples does Don Quinn give of ways other countries are trying to stop cheating?

   _____

   _____

   _____

B. Compare notes with a partner. Did you use the same abbreviations and symbols?

C. Read the paragraphs. Then listen again. Check (✓) the paragraph that best summarizes the main idea of the news report.

☐ 1. Many countries have problems with cheating. Some universities in China stop wireless phone messages, so students can't send text messages.

☐ 2. Cheating is a problem in many schools. New technology makes it easier to cheat. Schools and teachers are thinking of ways to stop cheating.

☐ 3. Teachers believe their students are honest, so they feel upset when students cheat. Students who cheat receive a zero on their work.

D. Complete the sentences in your own words using information from the listening.

1. According to a recent survey, _____ of U.S. high school students cheat in school.

2. Wendy Smith thinks that it is not possible to prevent students from

_____.

3. When Wendy Smith learned her students were cheating, she felt

_____.

4. Don Quinn thinks that the Internet is _____

_____.

5. Don Quinn and Wendy Smith disagree about the use of

_____.

E. The two teachers express different opinions about cheating and what teachers and schools should do to prevent it. Use phrases from the box to write each person's opinions. Write three sentences for each person.

> I think / I don't think . . .
> I feel that . . .
> In my opinion, . . .
> Students should / shouldn't . . .
> Schools should / shouldn't . . .

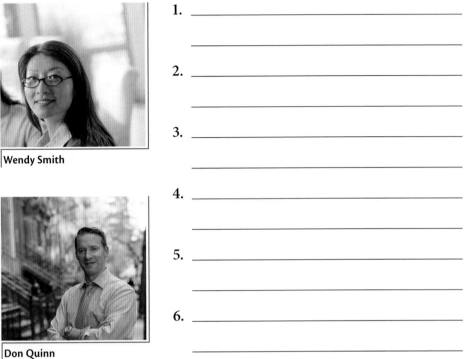

Wendy Smith

Don Quinn

1. _____
   _____

2. _____
   _____

3. _____
   _____

4. _____
   _____

5. _____
   _____

6. _____
   _____

F. Compare answers with a partner. Then share your sentences with the class.

SAY WHAT YOU THINK

Discuss the questions in a group.

1. According to the teachers in the news story, why is cheating bad?

2. Do you think cheating is a problem in schools? Why or why not?

3. Do you think it is possible to stop students from cheating? How?

Sometimes speakers don't give their opinions directly. To understand what a speaker thinks or feels about a topic, we need to "read between the lines," or use the context to decide what the speaker is really saying. We call this **making an inference**. For example, in Listening 1, one of the teachers is speaking about her students' cheating.

> Well, I didn't want to believe it at first. I thought my students were truthful.

She doesn't say directly how she felt about the cheating, but you can understand that she felt sad or upset.

You can also make inferences about people's attitudes by listening for tone of voice.

A. Listen to the excerpts from Listening 1. Circle the correct answer.

1. Wendy Smith . . .
   a. thinks technology is the cause of cheating.
   b. does not allow students to use the Internet.

2. Wendy Smith . . .
   a. doesn't believe her high school students.
   b. believes students who cheat will suffer.

3. Don Quinn . . .
   a. thinks it's OK to copy from the Internet.
   b. doesn't think his students cheat.

4. Don Quinn . . .
   a. doesn't think cheating is a big problem at the school.
   b. wants to put cameras in the classrooms.

5. Wendy Smith . . .
   a. disagrees with Don Quinn.
   b. thinks students shouldn't get grades.

B. Compare answers with a partner. Explain the reasons for your answers. What information helped you get the answers? Listen again if necessary.

iQ ONLINE　**C. Go online for more practice with making inferences.**

UNIT OBJECTIVE ▶▶▶▶ You are going to listen to two conversations. One conversation is about school, and one is about getting a job. As you listen to the conversations, gather information and ideas about when honesty is important.

PREVIEW THE LISTENING

Vocabulary Skill Review

In Unit 5, you learned about using the dictionary to find the right definition. Use your dictionary to find another definition for the vocabulary word *lie*. Write a sentence using that definition.

A. **VOCABULARY** Here are some words and phrases from Listening 2. Read the sentences. Circle the answer that best matches the meaning of each <u>underlined</u> word or phrase.

1. If you find money in the street, I think you should take it to the police, even if it's just <u>a little bit</u> of money.
   a. a large amount
   b. a small amount

2. I found a great article online. Is it OK to use part of it in my report? I don't want to use the whole article—just a <u>section</u> of it.
   a. a part of something
   b. all of something

3. Teachers don't really know how many of their students cheat. That's because many students cheat on tests, but they don't <u>get caught</u>.
   a. to be found doing something wrong
   b. to find a report on the Internet

4. Sorry, you can't park here. It's <u>illegal</u>. This is a no-parking zone.
   a. OK sometimes
   b. not allowed by law

5. I'll finish my final report this week. It's a 20-page paper, and I have 15 pages <u>so far</u>.
   a. until now
   b. last year

6. Police officers have a big <u>responsibility</u>. They have to keep the city and its people safe.
   a. a free-time activity
   b. an important job to do

7. To tell a <u>lie</u> is not an honest thing to do.
   a. something you say that you know is not true
   b. something you say to appreciate another person

B. Go online for more practice with the vocabulary.

C. **PREVIEW** You are going to listen to two conversations. One conversation is about school, and one is about getting a job. What are ways people are sometimes dishonest in those situations? Add two ideas to each list.

At school: *sharing test answers,* _____

_____

_____

Getting a job: *lying about your education,* _____

_____

_____

WORK WITH THE LISTENING

A. **LISTEN AND TAKE NOTES** Listen to the two conversations. On a separate sheet of paper, take notes on the way each person is dishonest. Use abbreviations and symbols when possible.

B. Compare notes with a partner. Discuss any differences.

C. Read the statements. Write *T* (true) or *F* (false). Then correct any false statements.

____ **1.** André and Daniela are classmates.

_____

____ **2.** André copied his report from one website.

_____

____ **3.** André did not know his actions were wrong.

_____

____ **4.** Stephen is applying for a job at a bookstore.

_____

_____ 5. In the past, Stephen was the manager of a restaurant.

_____

_____ 6. Stephen thinks he has the experience he needs to get the job.

_____

D. **Complete the sentences in your own words using information from the listening.**

1. André and Daniela are writing _____.

2. According to Daniela, it is not OK to copy _____

   _____.

3. Plagiarism is _____.

4. Stephen is being dishonest about _____.

5. Stephen thinks it is not a lie because _____.

E. **Compare answers with a partner. Explain what key words or phrases from the listening helped you get the answers. Listen again if necessary.**

F. **What do you think André and Stephen should do next? Write your opinions. Then compare your ideas in a group.**

André:_____

_____

_____

_____

Stephen:_____

_____

_____

_____

iQ ONLINE   **G.** **Go online to listen to *Are You Dishonest Online?* and check your comprehension.**

SAY WHAT YOU THINK

A. Discuss the questions in a group.

1. What is your opinion about these actions? Do you think they are wrong?
   - copying a report from the Internet
   - giving false information on a résumé

2. Is it always better to be honest? Explain.

B. Before you watch the video, discuss the questions in a group.

1. Do you think most people lie?

2. Give examples of situations when people lie in relationships, for example, parent/child, husband/wife, brother/sister, two best friends, etc.

iQ ONLINE

C. Go online to watch the video about lies and relationships. Then check your comprehension.

counterintuitive *(adj.)* the opposite of what you would expect or what seems to be obvious

eliminate *(v.)* to stop; to cause to go away

ethical *(adj.)* connected with beliefs about what is right or wrong

ethicist *(n.)* a person who specializes in the study of ethics (what is good and bad)

lubrication *(n.)* the process of making something work smoothly

VIDEO VOCABULARY

D. Think about the unit video, Listening 1, and Listening 2 as you discuss the questions.

1. Why do you think people sometimes cheat or are dishonest?

2. What is your opinion about these statements?

   a. It's OK to tell a lie when the truth might hurt someone's feelings.

   b. You have to be a little dishonest to be a successful person.

3. Do you think it's possible to eliminate lying in our society?

Percentages and **fractions** are different ways of talking about an amount that is part of a whole (*one half, 50 percent*). When you give survey results or facts from an article, it's helpful to understand and know how to say numbers in these ways.

You can express amounts as either percentages or fractions. Here are some common examples.

(25%)	twenty-five percent	=	(1/4)	a quarter/one quarter
(33%)	thirty-three percent	=	(1/3)	a third/one third
(50%)	fifty percent	=	(1/2)	a half/one half
(66%)	sixty-six percent	=	(2/3)	two thirds
(75%)	seventy-five percent	=	(3/4)	three quarters

A. Listen to excerpts from Listening 1. Complete the excerpts with the correct percentages or fractions. Use words, not numbers.

1. A recent survey in the U.S. found that about _____ _____ of high school students cheat in school. They share test answers, look at classmates' test papers, and send text messages with answers during a test. And according to the survey, more than _____ of students also copy reports from the Internet.

2. Last year, about _____ of my students turned in final reports that they copied from the Internet.

3. I read an article about what schools in other countries are doing. The article said that in one African country, the government canceled about _____ of test scores after students cheated on tests.

4. And a university in Europe did a survey on cheating. According to the survey, _____ of students answered that they cheated. So the university put cameras in all of its classrooms.

B. Rewrite each amount from Activity A. Use numbers (25%, 3/4, etc.).

1. _____

   _____

2. _____

3. _____

4. _____

iQ ONLINE **C.** Go online for more practice with percentages and fractions.

SPEAKING

UNIT OBJECTIVE ▶▶▶▶ At the end of this unit, you are going to survey your classmates about their opinions on honesty and dishonesty. Then you will report the survey results to the class. As you speak, you will need to refer to a source of information.

Grammar   Conjunctions *and* and *but*

You can use the **conjunction *and*** to join two ideas or add another idea.

> Seventy-five percent of high school students say they cheat,
> **and** more than half say they copy reports from the Internet.

The conjunction ***but*** connects two opposite ideas.

> Some people think it's OK to copy articles from the Internet,
> **but** plagiarism is wrong.

A. Complete the sentences with *and* or *but*. Then read your sentences to a partner.

1. Jane put false information on her résumé. It says she has a college degree, _____ she really doesn't.

2. Once I found a wallet on the bus. It didn't have any money in it, _____ it had a lot of credit cards. I took it to the police station, _____ they returned it to the owner.

3. It's OK to use sections of an Internet article in your paper, _____ you need to give the author's name, _____ you should also give the website where you found it.

4. I try to be honest all the time, _____ sometimes it's impossible.

5. Mr. Markus is a very good businessman. His products are excellent, _____ his prices are fair.

6. Students who cheat may do well on tests, _____ they may get good grades, _____ they don't learn anything.

7. You shouldn't lie about your experience to get a job. Your boss might find out, _____ you'll lose your job.

B. Circle *and* or *but*. Then complete each sentence with your own idea.

1. Some people say it's OK to be a little dishonest in business, (and /(but))

   <u>I do not think that is right</u>   .

2. He uses a younger photo of himself on his web page, (and / but)

   _____.

3. I found some money in the street, (and / but) _____

   _____.

4. She gave her homework to a classmate, (and / but) _____

   _____.

5. He lied about breaking the vase, (and / but) _____

   _____.

C. Read your sentences to a partner.

 D. Go online for more practice with the conjunctions *and* and *but*.

E. Go online for the grammar expansion.

Pronunciation	Linking consonants to vowels

Speakers often connect the sounds between words. This is called **linking**. One way they do this is by linking a word that ends in a consonant sound to a word after it that begins with a vowel sound.

 Listen to these phrases.

because of	quiz answers	false information
a third of	not acceptable	have a lot of

A. Listen to the sentences. Show the linked consonant and vowel sounds by connecting the letters.

1. I think a lot of people lie about their age.

2. Is it OK to keep money that you find in the street?

3. About a quarter of the students in the class cheated on the test.

4. Do you think it's OK to call in sick to work if you're not sick?

5. In our English class, it's not OK to use an article from the Internet without giving credit.

B. Work with a partner. Take turns reading the sentences from Activity A. Practice linking the consonant and vowel sounds.

iQ ONLINE **C. Go online for more practice with linking consonants to vowels.**

Speaking Skill | Sourcing information

Sometimes you need to include information that you get from the Internet, a newspaper or magazine article, a radio news report, or a survey. It's important to give this information the right way in research reports or class discussions. You must name the **source** of your information. Here are some useful phrases to refer to a source of information.

According to the	survey, article, website,	75 percent of students cheat.
The survey	found that	some people are honest.
The results	showed that	most people are honest.
More than half	answered	yes / no.
About 75 percent	said	that they sometimes lie.

A. Look at the survey below. Match the survey results on the right with the phrases on the left. (Make guesses.) Then listen and check your answers.

Tip for Success

To avoid plagiarism, always use quotation marks (". . .") around anything that comes directly from a text. Be sure to give the source.

Survey Results!

People surveyed . . .	do this!?
_____ 1. More than half	a. give false information on a résumé.
_____ 2. Over ten percent	b. sometimes change the price tag to a lower price for something they want to buy.
_____ 3. About 20%	c. take paper or pens from their company to use at home.
_____ 4. About 60%	d. sometimes lie to friends or family to avoid hurting their feelings.
_____ 5. Three quarters	e. call in sick to work when they aren't sick.

B. Work with a partner. Talk about the survey results in Activity A. Use the phrases from the Speaking Skill box on page 137.

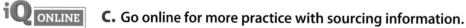

"The survey found that more than half of people . . ."

iQ ONLINE **C.** Go online for more practice with sourcing information.

UNIT OBJECTIVE ▶▶▶▶ In this assignment, you are going to survey your classmates about their opinions on honesty and dishonesty. Then you will report your survey results to the class. As you prepare your survey, think about the Unit Question, "When is honesty important?" Use information from Listening 1, Listening 2, the unit video, and your work in the unit to support your survey. Refer to the Self-Assessment checklist on page 140.

CONSIDER THE IDEAS

🔊 Listen to the beginning of Nasir's report on his honesty survey of his classmates. Fill in the blanks with the missing percentages.

Nasir Memon
Honesty Survey Report
English 101
Honesty Survey Results

1. How important do you think honesty is?

    ____% very important

    _36_% a little important

    ____% not important

2. Are you honest all the time?

    ____% yes ____% no

3. How wrong do you think these actions are?

    • not returning a library book

        ____% not wrong   _61_% a little wrong   ____% very wrong

    • hitting a car in a parking lot and not telling the owner

        ____% not wrong   _3_% a little wrong   ____% very wrong

    • cheating on a test

        _9_% not wrong   ____% a little wrong   ____% very wrong

---

PREPARE AND SPEAK

A. **GATHER IDEAS** Complete the activities.

1. Write five survey questions to ask your classmates about honesty. Use *yes/no* questions (as in number 2 of Nasir's survey) and multiple choice questions (as in numbers 1 and 3).

2. Work with a partner to test your questions. Ask your partner the questions and make changes if necessary.

B. **ORGANIZE IDEAS** Ask ten people your five survey questions. Record each person's answers. When you finish, count the number of answers for each question. Write your survey results as percentages.

C. **SPEAK** Work in a group. Report the results of your honesty survey. Use the percentages and fractions, and use phrases that source the results of your survey. Refer to the Self-Assessment checklist below before you begin.

 Go online for your alternate Unit Assignment.

CHECK AND REFLECT

A. **CHECK** Think about the Unit Assignment as you complete the Self-Assessment checklist.

SELF-ASSESSMENT		
Yes	**No**	
☐	☐	I was able to speak easily about the topic.
☐	☐	I used abbreviations and symbols to save time when taking notes.
☐	☐	My partner/group/class understood me.
☐	☐	I used *and* and *but* correctly.
☐	☐	I used vocabulary from the unit.
☐	☐	I used phrases to source information.
☐	☐	I linked consonants to vowels.

 B. **REFLECT** Go to the Online Discussion Board to discuss these questions.

1. What is something new you learned in this unit?

2. Look back at the Unit Question—When is honesty important? Is your answer different now than when you started the unit? If yes, how is it different? Why?

TRACK YOUR SUCCESS

Circle the words and phrases you have learned in this unit.

Nouns
grade 🔑 AWL
lie 🔑
responsibility 🔑
section 🔑 AWL
survey AWL
technology 🔑 AWL

Verbs
cheat 🔑
suffer 🔑

Adjective
illegal 🔑 AWL

Percentages and Fractions
a quarter 🔑
twenty-five percent
thirty-three percent
fifty percent
sixty-six percent
seventy-five percent

Phrases
a little bit
according to 🔑
get caught
so far
About 75 percent
said . . .
More than half
answered . . .
The results showed
that . . .
The survey found
that . . .

🔑 Oxford 2000 keywords
AWL Academic Word List

Check (✓) the skills you learned. If you need more work on a skill, refer to the page(s) in parentheses.

NOTE TAKING ▪	I can use abbreviations and symbols to save time when taking notes. (p. 123)
LISTENING ▪	I can make inferences. (p. 128)
VOCABULARY ▪	I can recognize and use percentages and fractions. (p. 133)
GRAMMAR ▪	I can recognize and use the conjunctions *and* and *but*. (p. 135)
PRONUNCIATION ▪	I can link consonants to vowels. (p. 136)
SPEAKING ▪	I can refer to a source of information. (p. 137)
UNIT OBJECTIVE ▶▶▶▶ ▪	I can gather information and ideas to conduct a survey on honesty and dishonesty, and then report my results to the class.

UNIT 7

Behavioral Science

LISTENING ▶	listening for different opinions
VOCABULARY ▶	verb-noun collocations
GRAMMAR ▶	imperative of *be* + adjective
PRONUNCIATION ▶	content word stress in sentences
NOTE TAKING ▶	using an outline
SPEAKING ▶	checking for listeners' understanding

UNIT QUESTION

Is it ever too late to change?

A Discuss these questions with your classmates.

1. Do you like to make changes in your life, or do you prefer things to stay the same?

2. Do you think old people or young people find it easier to make changes in their lives? Why?

3. Look at the photo. What kinds of changes do you think these people are making in their lives?

B Listen to *The Q Classroom* online. Then answer these questions.

1. Some of the students think it is difficult for older people to change. What reasons do they give?

2. Marcus feels it's never too late if you really want to change. Do you agree?

3. What was the last big change in your life? How difficult was it?

iQ ONLINE **C** Go to the Online Discussion Board to discuss the Unit Question with your classmates.

D Check (✓) the changes in your life. Write when each change happened. Then tell a partner about your changes. Were they easy or difficult for you?

Change	When it happened
☐ moved to a new house or apartment	
☐ changed schools	
☐ started high school	
☐ started college	
☐ moved to a new city or town	
☐ started a new job or career	
☐ stopped a bad habit	
☐ moved to a different country	
☐ got married	
☐ had a child	

E Look at the pictures. With a partner, describe the change the person is making. Why was it difficult at first? What did he do to make it better? Did you ever have a similar experience?

LISTENING

LISTENING 1 | Attitudes about Change

UNIT OBJECTIVE ▶▶▶▶ You are going to listen to a group of students discussing proverbs about change. As you listen to the conversation, gather information and ideas about whether it is ever too late to change.

PREVIEW THE LISTENING

A. **VOCABULARY** Here are some words and phrases from Listening 1. Read their definitions. Then complete each sentence below with the correct word or phrase.

> **accept** (*verb*) 🔑 to say yes to something
>
> **change your mind** (*phrasal verb*) to decide to do something differently; to change your plan
>
> **especially** (*adverb*) 🔑 more than usual or more than others
>
> **flexible** (*adjective*) able to change easily
>
> **opportunity** (*noun*) 🔑 a chance to do something
>
> **progress** (*noun*) 🔑 improvement or development
>
> **proverb** (*noun*) a popular saying that many people know and say, which teaches an important lesson
>
> **remain** (*verb*) 🔑 to stay the same way; not to change

🔑 Oxford 2000 keywords

Vocabulary Skill Review

In Unit 6, you learned about percentages and fractions. Can you find any percentages or fractions in Activity A? How do you say them?

1. My boss dislikes any kind of change. It's difficult for her to _____ new ideas.

2. Life changes can be difficult, _____ big changes like moving to a new country.

3. My school has a study abroad program in London. About two thirds of my class is going, and I'm definitely going to go, too. It's a really good _____ to improve my English.

4. Karen did much better in school this year. She studied hard and made _____ in all her classes. She just got 90 percent on her math test.

5. Greg hates any kind of change. He really needs to learn to be more _____.

6. I learned a Chinese _____ about change today. It says, "A journey of a thousand miles begins with one step."

7. Are you still planning to move to a new apartment this summer, or did you _____?

8. Everything changes. Nothing can _____ the same for very long.

iQ ONLINE **B.** Go online for more practice with the vocabulary.

C. **PREVIEW** You are going to listen to a group of international university students discussing proverbs about change. What do you think these proverbs mean?

Match each proverb with its meaning.

____ 1. Life is what you make it.

____ 2. Never say never.

____ 3. It's never too late to change.

____ 4. All change is progress.

a. You can change at any age if you want to.

b. You can do anything you want to in life.

c. You should always be open to change.

d. Change is always good.

WORK WITH THE LISTENING

A. **LISTEN AND TAKE NOTES** Listen to the conversation. Fill in the blanks with the missing information.

1. Andrew   **Country:** ___U.S.___

   Proverb: Never _____.

   Meaning: Always be _____.

2. Franco   **Country:** _____

   Proverb: One who does not look ahead, _____.

   Meaning: It's important to _____ new _____.

3. Juan Carlos   **Country:** _____

   Proverb: A wise man _____, but _____

   _____.

   Meaning: A person who cannot _____

   _____.

4. Katrina   **Country:** _____

   Proverb: To change and to _____ are two _____.

   Meaning: We should be careful when we _____. First,

   we should be sure the change _____.

B. Compare answers with a partner. Then talk about these proverbs and the ones on page 146. Which ones do you like? Are there similar proverbs in your country?

C. Read the statements. Listen again and write *T* (true) or *F* (false). Then write information from the students' conversation to explain your answers.

___ 1. Andrew, Franco, Juan Carlos, and Katrina are all from different countries.

_____

___ 2. The students agree with all of the proverbs.

_____

____ 3. They don't like to make changes in their lives.

_____

____ 4. Several of the students say they are happy they came to the United
States to study.

_____

____ 5. They are afraid to move to another country.

_____

D. **Some of the students express different opinions about change.
Complete their opinions in your own words.**

1. Andrew:

When people get older, _____.

2. Franco:

Everyone can _____.

It's important to _____.

3. Juan Carlos:

It's always _____.

4. Katrina:

When we make a change, we should _____.

5. Most students:

Coming to study in the U.S. _____.

Change is _____.

E. **Discuss your answers in a group. Which opinions do you agree with?**

SAY WHAT YOU THINK

Discuss the questions in a group.

Tip for Success

It's a good idea to learn proverbs, sayings, and expressions in English. They are used frequently in daily life.

1. Which proverb from the listening do you like best? Why?

2. What do most of the students agree is important for people to do if they want to improve their lives?

3. What do people think about change in your culture? Is it a positive thing or a negative thing? Do you agree?

Listening Skill | **Listening for different opinions**

People express different opinions when they speak. Listening for the phrases or expressions that a speaker uses will help you to know when a speaker is agreeing or disagreeing. If you learn these expressions, you can participate more easily in discussions and add your own opinions.

Agreement

When speakers agree with an opinion or idea, they often use these expressions.

I totally agree.	Me, too.	You're right.
I think so, too.	Definitely!	That's true.

Disagreement

Speakers sometimes disagree directly. But it is more common to use indirect expressions because they sound more polite.

Direct		**Indirect (more polite)**
I disagree.	→	I'm not sure I agree.
I don't think so.	→	I don't know if I agree.
That's not true.	→	I don't know about that.

 A. Listen to the excerpts from Listening 1. Write the missing expressions.

1. **Andrew:** When we get older, it's more difficult to change.

    Older people don't want to change their thinking or their lifestyle.

    They like things to stay the same.

    Franco: _____. I think older people *can*

    change. Everyone can change. It's important to be flexible at any age.

2. **Franco:** In Brazil, we say, "One who does not look ahead, remains behind." This means it's important to accept new ideas. You should always be ready to change.

 Professor: And what do you think, Juan Carlos?

 Juan Carlos: _____. In Spain, we say, "A wise man changes his mind, but a fool never will."

3. **Juan Carlos:** This means that a person who cannot change his or her way of thinking is a fool. But if you can change your mind and be flexible, it makes you a wise person.

 Professor: Katrina?

 Katrina: Hmm. _____. Change isn't *always* good.

4. **Katrina:** We should be careful when we change things. First, we should be sure the change will make things better.

 Franco: _____. The important thing is that we *can* change—I mean improve—if we want to.

B. **Discuss each statement with a partner. Agree or disagree using the expressions from the Listening Skill box on page 149. Give reasons for your opinion.**

1. Older people can't change.

2. People can't change their personalities.

3. Big life changes are stressful.

4. The world isn't changing for the better.

5. Change isn't always good.

6. If something works well, you shouldn't change it—even if you can improve it.

iQ ONLINE **C.** **Go online for more practice with listening for different opinions.**

You are going to listen to a radio call-in show with professional life coach Diana Carroll. As you listen to the program, gather information and ideas about whether it is ever too late to change.

PREVIEW THE LISTENING

A. VOCABULARY Here are some words and phrases from Listening 2. Read the sentences. Circle the answer that best matches the meaning of each <u>underlined</u> word or phrase.

1. Some <u>habits</u> are hard to change, for example, biting your fingernails or eating sweets.
   a. actions you dislike
   b. actions you do often

2. Many people want to lose weight. They may start a diet, but they often fail because they can't <u>stick to</u> it.
   a. to continue
   b. to begin

3. If you want to change the world, start with yourself. I think that's good <u>advice</u>.
   a. something that you say to help someone decide what to do
   b. something that you do to help someone

4. Can you <u>recommend</u> a good computer program for learning English?
   a. to teach someone about something
   b. to tell someone that a person or a thing is good or useful

5. I'm taking classes in web design. My <u>goal</u> is to start my own company someday.
   a. something that you don't like
   b. something that you want to do

6. I hope I don't forget our exercise class on Tuesday. Can you please call me to <u>remind</u> me about it?
   a. to help someone find something
   b. to help someone remember something

7. A good teacher should <u>encourage</u> students and help them improve.
   a. to help someone continue something
   b. to help someone stop something

8. Don't give up! If you work hard, you can <u>achieve</u> anything you want to.
   a. to do or finish
   b. to forget

 B. Go online for more practice with the vocabulary.

C. PREVIEW **You are going to listen to a radio call-in show with professional life coach Diana Carroll. What do you think a life coach does?**

_____

_____

WORK WITH THE LISTENING

A. Listen to the radio program. What kind of change does the caller ask for help with?

_____

_____

B. LISTEN AND TAKE NOTES **Listen again. Make an outline to list Diana Carroll's advice to the caller. Use Roman numerals for the steps, and use letters and numbers for the examples and details. Follow this example.**

> I. Set small goals.
>   A. not too many big changes quickly
>   B. small goals – better chance of success
>   C. exercise – short walk 2–3 days a week

C. Compare outlines with a partner. Discuss any differences in your notes.

Oxford 2000 keywords

D. Check (✓) the summary that best describes the radio call-in show.

WOUP Radio
Show Summary
August 16–21

☐ **1.** On today's show, life coach Diana Carroll talks about how she started her career and gives advice to people who want to become a life coach.

☐ **2.** This week, life coach Diana Carroll gives several callers advice about how to stop bad habits like overeating and watching too much TV.

☐ **3.** Life coach Diana Carroll joins the show. She tells us what a life coach does and helps one caller set goals to start a healthy lifestyle.

E. Match the sentence halves. Then compare answers with a partner.

____ **1.** A life coach

____ **2.** The caller

____ **3.** People who write down their goals

____ **4.** Telling your goal to someone can help you

____ **5.** You should be prepared to

____ **6.** When you achieve a goal, you should

a. celebrate your success.

b. achieve them more often.

c. stick to your plan.

d. change your goal or take more time.

e. helps people improve their lives.

f. works too much and wants to be healthier.

F. Imagine you are the next caller on the same radio show. What question will you ask? Write it down, and then share it with a partner. Give each other one piece of advice for how to achieve the goal.

Question: _____

 G. Go online to listen to *Changing Careers* and check your comprehension.

SAY WHAT YOU THINK

A. Discuss the questions in a group.

1. Did you ever try to change a habit? What was the habit? Were you successful?

2. What are some things you'd like to change in your life? Make notes. Then share your answers.

B. Before you watch the video, discuss the questions in a group.

1. How are you different now than in the past?

2. Describe an important experience you had that changed you or your thinking.

iQ ONLINE

C. Go online to watch the video about Barack Obama. Then check your comprehension.

> **VIDEO VOCABULARY**
>
> **destructive** *(adj.)* dangerous to yourself and others
>
> **role model** *(n.)* a person you admire and want to be like
>
> **serious** *(adj.)* thinking deeply

D. Think about the unit video, Listening 1, and Listening 2 as you discuss the questions.

1. Is it easy for you to make big changes in your life, for example, changing your home, school, or job? How do you feel when you make these types of changes?

2. Would you like to try using a life coach? Why or why not?

3. In the video, Barack Obama tells about a person who said, "It's not about you; it's about what you can do for other people." How do you think this affected him?

Collocations are words that you often find together. For example, certain verbs go together with certain nouns in collocations like *make changes* or *set a goal*. You can improve your vocabulary if you learn new collocations and use them when you speak.

Some verbs go together with different nouns.

Tip for Success

A collocations dictionary lists English collocations alphabetically for easy reference.

change	
change one's attitude	The car accident **changed her attitude** about life.
change one's mind	Did you **change your mind** about moving?
make	
make a change	I need to **make some changes** in my life.
make progress	Kelly is **making a lot of progress** in math.

Some nouns go together with several verbs.

advice	
follow advice	Abdullah didn't **follow his friend's advice**.
give advice	Parents often **give advice** to their children.
goal	
achieve a goal	If you work hard, you can **achieve any goal**.
set a goal	It's important to **set small goals**.

A. Read the excerpts from Listening 1 and Listening 2. Complete the collocations. Then listen and check your answers.

1. Some people want to make really big changes in their lives, for example, to find a new job or career, or to move to a new city. Others want to break bad habits, such as overeating or watching too much TV. And other people want to change their _____ about life in general—for example, they want to become more friendly or flexible.

2. You need to share your goal with someone—for example, a coworker or a friend . . . someone who can help you _____ your goal.

3. I give _____ to people who want to make changes in their lives.

4. In Spain, we say, "A wise man changes his _____, but a fool never will."

5. Many people want to change their lives, but they aren't sure how to get started. Or maybe they are able to make a _____, but they can't stick to it.

6. And we made a lot of _____ with our English. . . . That's definitely a change for the better!

7. Thank you so much. You really helped me today. I'm definitely going to follow your _____.

8. The first step is to set small _____ for yourself. Many people try to make too many big changes quickly.

B. Write five questions about change to ask a partner. Use one of the collocations from the Vocabulary Skill box on page 155 in each question.

1. _____

2. _____

3. _____

4. _____

5. _____

C. Take turns asking and answering your questions from Activity B with a partner.

iQ ONLINE **D.** Go online for more practice with verb-noun collocations.

SPEAKING

At the end of this unit, you are going to choose a topic and give your classmates advice for how to make a change in their lives. As you give your advice, you will need to check for listeners' understanding.

Grammar | Imperative of *be* + adjective

When you give advice to someone, you can use the **imperative** of *be* + adjective. The imperative is the same as the base form of the verb.

☐ **Be** ready.   **Be** careful.

When you give negative advice, use ***don't be*** + **adjective**.

☐ **Don't be** afraid.

To give more detailed advice, you can add ***to*** + **infinitive** to many adjectives.

⌐ Be ready **to change** your goals.
  imperative adjective infinitive
└ Be careful **to check** your progress.   Don't be afraid **to ask** for advice.

A. Write advice about how to be a better English student. Use *be* (or *don't be*) + adjective + infinitive. Then share your advice with a partner. Use the adjectives in the box or your own ideas.

afraid	careful	prepared	ready	sure

1. _____

2. _____

3. _____

4. _____

5. _____

B. Read the article about how to start a new career. <u>Underline</u> the examples of *be* + adjective.

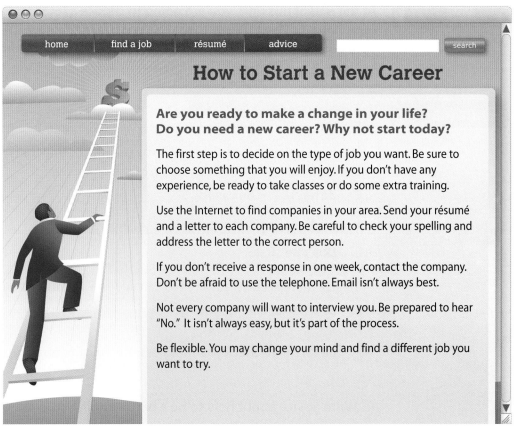

How to Start a New Career

Are you ready to make a change in your life?
Do you need a new career? Why not start today?

The first step is to decide on the type of job you want. Be sure to choose something that you will enjoy. If you don't have any experience, be ready to take classes or do some extra training.

Use the Internet to find companies in your area. Send your résumé and a letter to each company. Be careful to check your spelling and address the letter to the correct person.

If you don't receive a response in one week, contact the company. Don't be afraid to use the telephone. Email isn't always best.

Not every company will want to interview you. Be prepared to hear "No." It isn't always easy, but it's part of the process.

Be flexible. You may change your mind and find a different job you want to try.

C. Work with a partner. Imagine you are a life coach. Take turns giving the advice from Activity B. Look at the article if you need to, but be sure to make eye contact with your partner.

D. Go online for more practice with the imperative of *be* + adjective.

E. Go online for the grammar expansion.

Pronunciation | Content word stress in sentences

Content words are the words that have the most meaning in a sentence. They are usually *nouns*, *main verbs*, *adverbs*, and *adjectives*. We usually stress the content words in a sentence. We say the stressed words a little more loudly and strongly than the other words in the sentence. In the proverbs below, the content words are bold.

Listen and pay attention to the word stress.

1. **Life** is what you **make** of it.
2. Be the **change** you **want** to see in the **world**.
3. It's **never** too **late** to **change**.
4. To **change** and to **improve** are two **different things**.

A. Circle the content words in these proverbs. Then listen and check the stress.

1. To learn is to change.

2. A change is as good as a rest.

3. Change your thoughts, and you change your world.

4. To improve is to change; to be perfect is to change often.

5. You change your life by changing your heart.

B. Listen again and repeat the proverbs in Activity A. Then discuss the meaning of the proverbs with a partner.

iQ ONLINE **C.** Go online for more practice with content word stress in sentences.

In Unit 5, you learned how to use a numbered list to organize your notes. An **outline** uses both numbers and letters to organize main points and smaller details. Teachers often require students to write outlines when they are researching and preparing to write essays or give presentations.

Use Roman numerals, I., II., III., etc., for the most important points/topics.

Use capital letters, A., B., C., etc., for subpoints/subtopics.

Use numbers, 1., 2., 3., etc., for smaller examples or details.

Look at a student's notes for her book report as you listen to the beginning of her book report presentation.

Book Report Outline

The Art of Change by Archer Parks

I. Section 1 – Before the Change – how to prepare

   A. Chapter 1 – Making a Choice

      1. how to decide what habit to change

      2. people often try to change too many things – choose one

   B. Chapter 2 – The Tools of Change – things to help with success

      1. a friend or family member to encourage you

      2. a notebook or journal

A. Listen to the rest of the book report. Complete the rest of the outline.

> II. Section 2 – _____
> A. Chapter 1 – _____
>   1. importance of writing down goals
>   2. recommends _____
> B. _____
>   1. ideas for how to _____
>   2. it is normal to _____
>   3. "Don't think of it _____."

B. Compare outlines with a partner.

 C. Go online for more practice with using an outline.

Speaking Skill **Checking for listeners' understanding**

> When you give instructions or an explanation, it's helpful to stop and check that the listener understands everything. Here are some expressions you can use to check other people's understanding.
>
> > Does everyone understand?
> > Does that make sense?
> > Is that clear?
> > Are there any questions?

 for Success

It's polite to acknowledge an audience member's question before you answer it. Speakers often use expressions like *That's an excellent question. / Thank you for asking that. / Good question.*

A. Look back at Activity A on page 157. Think about places where you can stop to check for listeners' understanding.

B. Work in a group. Take turns giving your instructions for how to be a better English student. Remember to stop and check for listeners' understanding.

 C. Go online for more practice with checking for listeners' understanding.

UNIT OBJECTIVE ▶▶▶▶

In this assignment, you are going to choose a topic and give your classmates instructions on how to make a specific change in their lives. As you prepare your instructions, think about the Unit Question, "Is it ever too late to change?" Use information from Listening 1, Listening 2, the unit video, and your work in the unit to help you prepare your instructions. Refer to the Self-Assessment checklist on page 164.

CONSIDER THE IDEAS

Listen to James's instructions for how to break the habit of watching too much TV. Number the steps in the correct order.

How to Break the Habit of Watching Too Much TV

____ Add one more activity into your schedule every week.

____ Write a list of other activities you like to do.

____ Choose one or two hours when you usually watch TV. Write down a different activity.

____ Set a goal to watch less TV.

____ Celebrate when you achieve your goal.

____ Make a TV schedule.

PREPARE AND SPEAK

A. GATHER IDEAS Complete the activities.

1. Choose a topic from this list or think of your own topic. Start taking notes by writing your topic.

   - Good habits (How to start . . .)
   - Bad habits (How to stop . . .)
   - Personality traits (How to be more/less . . .)
   - New skills/hobbies/sports (How to start/learn . . .)
   - New jobs (How to become . . .)
   - Other:

   _____

2. Complete a graphic organizer with ideas for your topic. As an example, here is James's graphic organizer for how to break the habit of watching too much TV.

B. ORGANIZE IDEAS Use the information from your word web to create an outline for your presentation. List advice and instructions for how to make the change.

C. **SPEAK** Complete the activities. Refer to the Self-Assessment checklist below before you begin.

1. Practice with a partner. Take turns giving your instructions. Check your partner's understanding.

2. Work in a group. Take turns giving your instructions. Use your outline from Activity B if you need to, but make eye contact as much as possible.

 Go online for your alternate Unit Assignment.

CHECK AND REFLECT

A. **CHECK** Think about the Unit Assignment as you complete the Self-Assessment checklist.

SELF-ASSESSMENT		
Yes	No	
☐	☐	I was able to speak easily about the topic.
☐	☐	I used an outline for my notes.
☐	☐	My partner/group/class understood me.
☐	☐	I used the imperative of *be* + adjective correctly.
☐	☐	I used vocabulary from the unit.
☐	☐	I checked for understanding.
☐	☐	I stressed content words in sentences.

 B. **REFLECT** Go to the Online Discussion Board to discuss these questions.

1. What is something new you learned in this unit?

2. Look back at the Unit Question—Is it ever too late to change? Is your answer different now than when you started the unit? If yes, how is it different? Why?

TRACK YOUR SUCCESS

Circle the words, phrases, and expressions you have learned in this unit.

Nouns
advice 🔑
goal 🔑 AWL
habit 🔑
opportunity 🔑
progress 🔑
proverb

Verbs
accept 🔑
achieve 🔑 AWL
encourage 🔑
recommend 🔑
remain 🔑
remind 🔑

Phrasal Verbs
change your mind
stick to

Adjective
flexible AWL

Adverb
especially 🔑

Collocations
achieve a goal
change your attitude
follow advice
give advice
make a change
make progress
set a goal

Expressions
I (totally) agree.
You're right.
I think so, too.
That's true.
Me, too.
Definitely! AWL
I disagree.
I'm not sure I agree.
I don't think so.
I don't know if I agree.
That's not true.
I don't know about that.
Does that make sense?
Does everyone
  understand?
Is that clear?
Are there any questions?

🔑 Oxford 2000 keywords
AWL Academic Word List

Check (✓) the skills you learned. If you need more work on a skill, refer to the page(s) in parentheses.

LISTENING ■	I can listen for different opinions. (p. 149)
VOCABULARY ■	I can recognize and use verb-noun collocations. (p. 155)
GRAMMAR ■	I can recognize and use the imperative of *be* + adjective. (p. 157)
PRONUNCIATION ■	I can use content word stress in sentences. (p. 159)
NOTE TAKING ■	I can use an outline when taking notes. (p. 160)
SPEAKING ■	I can check for listeners' understanding. (p. 161)
UNIT OBJECTIVE ▶▶▶▶ ■	I can gather information and ideas to give instructions on how people can make a change in their lives.

NOTE TAKING	▶	using the Cornell method for taking notes
LISTENING	▶	listening for examples
VOCABULARY	▶	idioms and expressions
GRAMMAR	▶	*so* and *such* with adjectives
PRONUNCIATION	▶	linking vowel sounds with /w/ or /y/
SPEAKING	▶	expressing emotion

Q ?

UNIT QUESTION

When is it good to be afraid?

A Discuss these questions with your classmates.

1. What kinds of things make you feel afraid?

2. Do you enjoy the feeling of fear, for example, when you watch a horror movie or ride on a fast theme-park ride?

3. Look at the photo. What is the diver doing? Do you think this person is afraid?

UNIT
OBJECTIVE ▶▶▶▶ Listen to a presentation and a conversation. Gather
information and ideas to describe a frightening
experience.

◎ **B** **Listen to *The Q Classroom* online. Then answer these questions.**

1. What examples of fears do the students discuss?

2. Felix says it's good to be afraid of things that can actually hurt us, like dangerous sports. Can you think of other examples?

3. Sophy says fear can keep us safe. What are other reasons fear can be good?

iQ ONLINE **C** **Go online to watch the video about cats and mice. Then check your comprehension.**

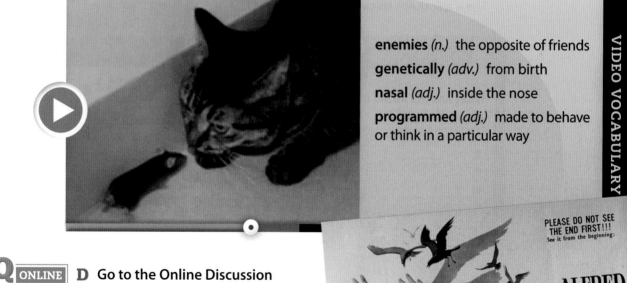

iQ ONLINE **D** **Go to the Online Discussion Board to discuss the Unit Question with your classmates.**

PLEASE DO NOT SEE
THE END FIRST!!!
See it from the beginning.

could be
the most
terrifying
motion
picture
I have
ever made!"

ALFRED HITCHCOCK'S
"The Birds"
TECHNICOLOR
Based on Daphne Du Maurier's classic suspense story!

ROD TAYLOR · JESSICA TANDY · SUZANNE PLESHETTE
and introducing 'TIPPI' HEDREN

167

E These pictures show common fears many people have. Check (✓) the things you are afraid of. Then discuss your answers with a partner.

insects and/or snakes

speaking in public

public transportation

closed spaces

high places

storms

F Ask five classmates about their worst fear from Activity E. Then ask them to say one more thing they are afraid of.

What are you afraid of ?		
Classmate's name	Worst fear from activity	Another fear
1.		
2.		
3.		
4.		
5.		

G Work in a group. Discuss these questions.

1. Do you and your classmates have the same fears? How are they the same? How are they different?

2. What is one thing a classmate is afraid of that you aren't? Do you understand this fear?

3. Do you think people learn to be afraid of things, or do you think people are born that way?

There are many different ways to take notes. One very useful method was developed at Cornell University by Professor Walter Pauk. You can use this method for any class or subject.

To use the **Cornell method**, start by drawing lines on a piece of paper to create three areas.

- Make a narrow column on the left for questions and key words.

- Make a wider note-taking column on the right.

- At the bottom of the page, leave space for a summary.

During the lecture or while you are reading, take notes on all the important information and details in the right-hand column. Use abbreviations and symbols where possible to keep the notes short.

When you finish, use the left-hand column to write key words or questions that will help you find information in the notes. Then, at the bottom, use your notes to write a few sentences to summarize the lecture/text.

Read the text about the author Stephen King. Then read the student's notes about the article for a creative writing class on page 170.

Anyone who enjoys reading scary stories knows the name Stephen King. He is the author of some the most famous horror novels of our time, such as *Christine* and *The Stand*. His books sell millions of copies worldwide.

King's early life was not easy. He was born in Portland, Maine on September 21, 1947. Stephen's father left the family when he was just two years old, so his mother raised Stephen and his brother David on her own. The family moved from place to place, wherever their mother could find work to support them.

David helped Stephen get his start in writing. In 1959, David started a small local newspaper called *Dave's Rag*. David told Stephen he could write reviews of books and TV shows for *Dave's Rag*. Stephen enjoyed the writing, and he felt like he was good at it. Soon he started writing his own scary stories and selling them to his classmates at school.

<table>
<tr><td colspan="2">Creative Writing Homework, Stephen King article</td></tr>
<tr><td>Questions/Key words</td><td>Notes</td></tr>
<tr><td>Who is Stephen King?</td><td>1 of mst famous horror authrs of all time</td></tr>
<tr><td>Early life</td><td>born in Portland, Maine, USA, 1947 not easy – father left when 2 yrs. old mother raised Stephen, brthr David – often moved</td></tr>
<tr><td>How did he start writing?</td><td>David strted nwspper, Dave's Rag Stephen wrote book, TV show reviews began to write scary stories, sold to clssmtes</td></tr>
</table>

Summary: *Stephen King is a famous horror author. He was born in Portland, Maine in 1947. His mother raised Stephen + his brother David on her own. Stephen wrote for David's newspaper, Dave's Rag. He started writing scary stories + sold them at school.*

A. Read the rest of the article below. Prepare a sheet of paper for taking notes using the Cornell method. Complete the *Notes* column. Then go back and complete the *Questions/Key words* and the *Summary*.

King's first novel almost didn't happen. One day, his wife Tabitha found a stack of papers in the trash. It was the book her husband was working on, called *Carrie*. She took it out of the trash can and told Stephen not to give up. He worked on it some more, and a major publishing company accepted it in 1974. The book was an instant success, and King's career as a successful writer began. He has written more than 30 horror novels, selling millions of copies each.

Although Stephen King writes about scary topics, he also has many fears. The writer whose books scare millions of people says he is afraid of rats, snakes, and even the dark!

B. Compare notes with a partner.

C. Go online for more practice with using the Cornell method for taking notes.

LISTENING

LISTENING 1 | The Science of Fear

UNIT OBJECTIVE ▶▶▶▶ You are going to listen to a conference presentation called "The Science of Fear." The speaker will discuss different types of fear, the body's reaction to fear, and the purpose of fear. As you listen to the presentation, gather information and ideas about when it is good to be afraid.

PREVIEW THE LISTENING

A. VOCABULARY Here are some words and phrases from Listening 1. Read their definitions. Then complete each sentence below with the correct word or phrase.

> **anxiety** (*noun*) a general feeling of worry or fear
>
> **get over** (*phrasal verb*) to become well or happy again after a difficult time or sickness
>
> **panic** (*verb*) to get a sudden feeling of fear that you cannot control
>
> **phobia** (*noun*) a very strong fear of something
>
> **purpose** (*noun*) 🔑 the reason for something
>
> **strength** (*noun*) 🔑 physical power
>
> **sweat** (*verb*) 🔑 to have liquid come from your skin, often because you are hot

🔑 Oxford 2000 keywords

Vocabulary Skill Review

In Unit 7, you learned about verb-noun collocations. Can you find any verb-noun collocations in Activity A? Circle them.

1. You should join a karate class. It will help you build _____. It could even change your attitude about life.

2. Lucia has a _____ of spiders. She saw one in her bedroom last month, and now she won't sleep there anymore.

3. I get nervous when I fly. I start to _____, even if I'm not very hot.

4. My first experience with public speaking was so terrible. I don't think I will ever _____ it.

5. Many students hate taking tests. They don't understand the _____ of them, and they don't think they are necessary.

6. If there is a fire, the important thing is not to _____.

Stay calm and walk, don't run, to the nearest exit.

7. Many people feel _____ about the future. They worry a lot

about our environment.

 B. Go online for more practice with the vocabulary.

C. PREVIEW You are going to listen to a conference presentation called "The Science of Fear." In this presentation, the speaker will discuss different types of fear, the body's reaction to fear, and the purpose of fear.

What do you think the speaker will say is the basic purpose of fear? Check (✓) your answer.

☐ It helps protect us from dangerous situations.
☐ It helps us feel less pain when we are hurt.

WORK WITH THE LISTENING

A. LISTEN AND TAKE NOTES Listen to the presentation. Complete the *Notes* column.

Presentation: The Science of Fear	
Questions/Key words	Notes emotion (happiness, sadness, love) feel when _____ diffrnt people afraid of diffrnt thngs
	anxiety (worry) – common fear abt something may happn in future
	panic – _____
	phobia – _____
	_____
	Imp*: Fear isn't _____.
	Some people _____.

When you 1st feel fear – _____

_____

Body gets _____

might hear _____

body _____

may be able to do amzing thngs, for ex, _____

_____

_____

Many stories abt _____

_____

Summary:

  B. Compare notes with a partner. Then work together to complete the
Questions/Key words column and write a short summary. Listen again
if needed. Read your summary to the class.

C. Read the statements. Write *T* (true) or *F* (false). Then correct any
false statements.

____ 1. Fear is different from other emotions, like happiness or sadness.

____ 2. There are several different types of fear.

____ 3. Most people are afraid of flying.

____ 4. Fear causes many changes in the body.

____ 5. Fear helps protect us from danger.

____ 6. Fear is always a bad feeling.

D. Circle the correct information to complete each sentence.

1. The situations that make us feel fear are (the same / different) for everyone.

2. One of the most common anxieties is about (money / snakes).

3. Panic is a (small / strong) type of fear.

4. People can sometimes get over (fear / phobias) with the help of a doctor.

5. Fear causes the brain to (move faster / make chemicals).

6. When we feel fear, our bodies get (warmer / colder).

7. Our bodies feel (strong and tight / weak and tired) when we feel fear.

8. Fear sometimes causes people to have amazing (dreams / strength).

E. Read the statements. Which type of fear is the person describing? Write *A* (anxiety), *Pa* (panic), or *Ph* (phobia).

____ 1. I can't go onstage now! I forgot the words to all the songs!

____ 2. I'm very worried about next year. I'm afraid I won't graduate.

____ 3. I *hate* mice. If I see one, I can't sleep for weeks.

____ 4. I always feel stressed about money. I'm afraid I won't have enough.

____ 5. My neighbor just got a pet snake. I think I have to move.

____ 6. Help! I can't get down from this ladder! I can't move.

SAY WHAT YOU THINK

Discuss the questions in a group.

1. In the presentation, the speaker discusses three types of fear: anxiety, panic, and phobia. Do you have these types of fears? If yes, what about?

   anxiety: _____

   panic: _____

   phobia: _____

2. The presenter says that sometimes people *enjoy* the feeling of fear such as when they watch a horror program. Can you think of other examples?

   _____ skydiving _____   _____

   _____ riding a roller coaster _____   _____

a roller coaster

Speakers often give **examples** to help make information clearer and to make a lecture or presentation more interesting. Listening for examples can often help you understand better and enjoy a presentation or lecture more.

Listen for the following words and phrases that signal examples.

| for example | like |
| for instance | such as |

A. Listen to the excerpts and continuation of the presentation in Listening 1. Listen for the examples and write them down.

Excerpt 1

1. Examples of emotions

_____

2. Example of a situation that makes people feel fear

_____

Excerpt 2

3. Examples of animals that cause phobias

_____

4. Examples of situations that cause phobias

_____

Excerpt 3

5. Examples of amazing things people do when they feel fear

_____

Excerpt 4

6. Examples of things people do because they want to feel fear

_____

iQ ONLINE   **B.** Go online for more practice with listening for examples.

LISTENING 2 | What Are You Afraid Of?

You are going to listen to a woman talk to her doctor about her fear of high places. As you listen to the conversation, gather information and ideas about when it is good to be afraid.

PREVIEW THE LISTENING

Tip for Success

Go back and review your notes within 24 hours of taking them. Rewrite any words or sections that you can't read or that don't make sense.

A. **VOCABULARY** Here are some words and phrases from Listening 2. Read the sentences. Circle the answer that best matches the meaning of each <u>underlined</u> word or phrase.

1. Some people are afraid of snakes, but snakes don't <u>bother</u> me. I like them.
   a. to annoy or worry somebody
   b. to understand clearly

2. John is <u>terrified</u> of closed spaces. It's too scary for him to ride in elevators or cars.
   a. very happy
   b. very afraid

3. I didn't sleep much last night. I had a <u>nightmare</u>. I thought there were spiders all over me.
   a. bad dream
   b. bad job

4. Ken hates high places. He prefers to stay close to the <u>ground</u>.
   a. front of a building
   b. surface of the Earth

5. Maria's fear of heights is completely <u>normal</u>. Many people have this fear.
   a. usual
   b. special

6. A lot of people have <u>negative</u> feelings about spiders.
   a. bad
   b. good

7. Jim loves speaking in public. He is the <u>ideal</u> person for the sales position.
   a. normal
   b. perfect

8. Public speaking can be scary at first, but after you give a few presentations, you <u>get used to</u> it.
   a. begin to feel comfortable
   b. become more afraid

iQ ONLINE **B.** Go online for more practice with the vocabulary.

C. **PREVIEW** You are going to listen to a woman talking to a doctor about her phobia of high places. Do you believe it is possible to get over a phobia?

🔑 Oxford 2000 keywords

WORK WITH THE LISTENING

A. **LISTEN AND TAKE NOTES** Prepare a sheet of paper for taking notes using the Cornell method. Listen to the conversation and complete the *Notes* column.

B. Listen again and add any important information to your notes. Then complete the *Questions/Key words* column and write a short summary of the conversation.

C. Compare notes with a partner. Discuss any differences.

D. Read the statements. Then check (✓) the four reasons Marcie came to the doctor.

    ☐ 1. She wants to stop having nightmares.

    ☐ 2. She plans to live in a tall building.

    ☐ 3. She wants to do more things with her friends.

    ☐ 4. She hopes to find a new job.

    ☐ 5. She wants to go rock climbing with her boss.

    ☐ 6. She wants to have a normal life.

E. Marcie talks about the negative effects of her phobia. Write a sentence to explain how her phobia affects each part of her life.

1. her health: _____

2. her hobbies: _____

3. her friendships: _____

4. her career: _____

_____

F. Read the questions. Then circle the correct answer.

1. How many times did Marcie visit Doctor Travis?
   a. This is her first visit.
   b. This is her second visit.
   c. She visits her often.

2. About how old was Marcie when her phobia started?
   a. 10 years old
   b. 12 years old
   c. 20 years old

3. What was her nightmare about?
   a. jumping off a tall building
   b. climbing a tall building
   c. falling off a tall building

4. What makes Marcie feel afraid?
   a. the tops of tall buildings
   b. only very high places, like buildings and bridges
   c. any place above the ground

5. How does Marcie feel about her phobia?
   a. She is upset about it.
   b. She is afraid of it.
   c. She is positive about it.

6. Why didn't Marcie take the ideal job?
   a. Because she would have to drive across a bridge.
   b. Because she didn't like the boss of the company.
   c. Because her friends invited her rock climbing.

7. Does the doctor think Marcie can get over her phobia?
   a. No.
   b. Yes.
   c. She doesn't know.

8. According to the doctor, what can you do to get over a phobia?
   a. avoid the things that scare you
   b. look at pictures of people who have phobias
   c. stop avoiding the things that scare you

iQ ONLINE **G.** Go online to listen to *Conquering Fears* and check your comprehension.

SAY WHAT YOU THINK

A. Discuss the questions in a group.

1. Do you think Marcie will be successful at getting over her phobia? Why or why not?

2. Do you know anyone with a phobia? What kind of phobia? Is that person doing anything to get over the phobia? If so, what is he or she doing?

B. Think about the unit video, Listening 1, and Listening 2 as you discuss the questions.

1. What are some ways that fear can be good and bad in our lives? Write your ideas in the T-chart.

Ways fear can be good	Ways fear can be bad

2. Why do you think some fears are good and others are bad?

Vocabulary Skill | **Idioms and expressions**

Idioms and expressions are phrases or sentences that have a special meaning. These phrases or sentences can be difficult to understand because you cannot easily guess the meaning, even if you know all of the words. Speakers often use idioms and expressions, so it's important to learn them.

Idiom or expression	Meaning
Please, **have a seat**.	Sit down.
Go ahead, **I'm all ears**.	I'm listening carefully.

Dictionaries
frequently include
idioms along with the
regular definitions
of a word. They
are often labeled
as *idiom* or *idm*.

A. Work with a partner. Read the sentences from Listening 2. <u>Underline</u> the idiom in each sentence.

1. When I woke up, I was sweating and <u>shaking like a leaf</u>.

2. I can't stand being up above the ground.

3. You can say that again. It really makes my life difficult.

4. So, I guess I'll just keep the job I have—even though my boss drives me crazy.

5. You may have a hard time looking at the photos at first.

6. You will get used to it before you know it.

B. Match each idiom from Activity A with the correct meaning.

a. makes someone feel annoyed or angry

b. very quickly

c. unable to control your body's movement because you feel very afraid

d. have difficulty

e. don't like at all

f. you're right

____ 1. shaking like a leaf

____ 2. can't stand

____ 3. You can say that again.

____ 4. drives me crazy

____ 5. have a hard time

____ 6. before you know it

iQ ONLINE **C.** Go online for more practice with idioms and expressions.

SPEAKING

UNIT OBJECTIVE ▶▶▶▶ At the end of this unit, you are going to tell your classmates about a time when you were in a frightening or dangerous situation. As you speak, you will need to express emotion.

Grammar | *So* and *such* with adjectives

We use *so* and *such* with adjectives to express a stronger feeling than the adjective by itself.

We usually use *so* + **adjective**.

I was **so scared**! (I was very scared!)

We use *such* + *a/an* + **adjective** + **singular noun**.

It was **such a loud noise**! (It was a very loud noise!)

We use *such* + **adjective** + **plural noun**.

They were **such scary programs**! (They were very scary programs!)

A. Complete each sentence with *so* or *such*.

1. The spider was _____ big that I thought it was a mouse.

2. The apartment was on _____ a high floor that I couldn't live there.

3. I was _____ nervous that my knees were shaking.

4. Lama is _____ afraid of snakes that she can't even look at a picture of one.

5. The rat had _____ sharp teeth that it could bite through wood.

6. I hid under my bed covers because it was _____ a bad storm.

7. May was _____ tired that she slept through the horror program.

8. My brother had _____ a hard time getting used to the small elevator in his building.

 | Listening and Speaking   **181**

B. Write sentences with *so* or *such* + the words or phrases in parentheses.

1. I was so scared!
    (scared)

2. _____
    (a big snake)

3. _____
    (a scary program)

4. _____
    (afraid of public speaking)

5. _____
    (worried)

6. _____
    (a long flight)

7. _____
    (loud)

8. _____
    (an important test)

C. Take turns reading your sentences aloud with a partner.

iQ ONLINE   **D.** Go online for more practice with *so* and *such* with adjectives.

E. Go online for the grammar expansion.

Pronunciation | Linking vowel sounds with /w/ or /y/

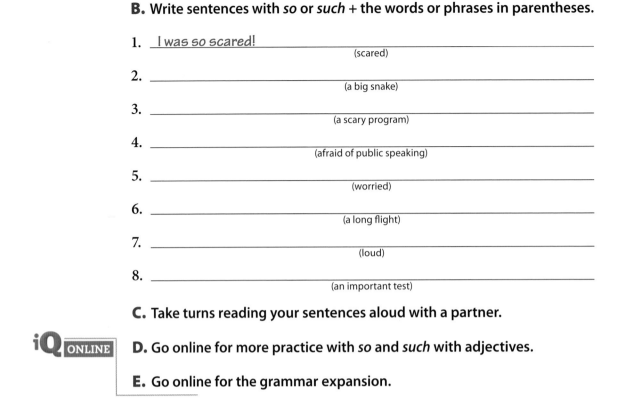

When a word ends with a vowel sound and the next word begins with a vowel sound, we link the words with /w/ or /y/.

Linking vowel sounds with /w/

If our lips are round at the end of the first word (as with /o/ or /u/ sounds), we link another word beginning with a vowel with /w/.

Listen to these phrases.

you are   who is   go up
  w   w   w

Linking vowel sounds with /y/

If our lips are wide at the end of the first word (as with /i/, /e/, or /a/ sounds), we link another word beginning with a vowel with /y/.

Listen to these phrases.

I am   she is   we aren't
  y   y   y

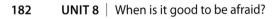

A. Underline the pair of words in each sentence where the first word ends with a vowel sound, and the second word begins with a vowel sound. Then write the correct linking sound, /w/ or /y/.

/w/ 1. Are <u>you afraid</u> of bats?

____ 2. Why are you scared of snakes?

____ 3. Julio is afraid of high places.

____ 4. She always screams when she hears thunder.

____ 5. Do you know anyone here?

____ 6. He is making me nervous.

____ 7. I don't see anyone I know here.

____ 8. I know three other people who have a phobia of closed spaces.

B. Listen to the sentences. Check your answers. Then take turns reading the sentences aloud with a partner.

iQ ONLINE **C.** Go online for more practice with linking vowel sounds with /w/ or /y/.

Speaking Skill Expressing emotion

Part of having a conversation is listening and responding. It's important to know *how* to respond to different types of information. It shows other people that you are listening and interested in what they are saying. Here are some expressions you can use to react to what someone tells you.

Expressing surprise	Expressing happiness	Expressing sadness
No kidding!	I'm glad to hear that.	I'm sorry to hear that.
No way!	That's wonderful.	That's terrible!
Are you serious?	Super.	How awful.

A. Read the conversations. Circle the expression that best completes each conversation.

1. **A:** I'm really afraid of bears.

   B: (No kidding! / I'm glad to hear that.) I think they're beautiful animals.

2. **A:** Birds scare me. I'm always afraid they are going to land on me.

   B: Oh, I love birds. I had four birds at home, but one of them died last month.

   A: (Super. / I'm sorry to hear that.)

3. **A:** I just gave a speech to everyone in my school!

   B: I thought you were afraid of public speaking.

   A: I was afraid, but I spent a lot of time practicing with small groups and I got over my fear!

   B: (That's wonderful. / That's terrible!)

4. **A:** How is your brother?

   B: He's not doing very well.

   A: Why not?

   B: You know, he's a very nervous person. He's afraid of loud noises, and his new neighbor is really loud!

   A: (I'm glad to hear that. / How awful.)

5. **A:** What do you think of spiders? Are you afraid of them?

   B: Yeah, I'm really afraid of spiders! I was bitten by one once!

   A: (I'm sorry to hear that. / No way!) How did that happen?

   B: It was on my arm, and I didn't see it.

B. Use the expressions from the Speaking Skill box on page 183 to complete the conversations. Different answers are possible. Then take turns reading the conversations aloud with a partner.

1. **A:** I heard a loud noise in the kitchen last night when I was home alone. It sounded like a scream. I was so scared.

   B: _____ What was it?

   A: It was just my cat! He was stuck behind the refrigerator, and he couldn't get out! He's OK now.

   B: _____

2. **A:** I read a scary book last month, and now I have nightmares every night.

   B: _____

A: That's OK. The dreams gave me an idea for a story. Now I'm writing a book!

B: _____

3. **A:** My company is moving its head office.

   B: _____ Where is it moving to?

   A: Well, it's going to be on the 60th floor of a building downtown. I can't work there anymore because I'm afraid of high places!

   B: _____

iQ **ONLINE** **C.** Go online for more practice with expressing emotion.

Unit Assignment | **Tell a personal story**

UNIT OBJECTIVE ▶▶▶▶ In this assignment, you are going to tell your classmates about a time when you were in a frightening or dangerous situation. You can also choose to talk about someone you know. As you prepare your story, think about the Unit Question, "When is it good to be afraid?" Use information from Listening 1, Listening 2, the unit video, and your work in the unit to support your story. Refer to the Self-Assessment checklist on page 186.

CONSIDER THE IDEAS

Listen to Mark tell his story to his friend. Then complete the chart.

When and where it happened	Who was there	What happened
How they felt	**What they did**	**How the story ended**

PREPARE AND SPEAK

A. **GATHER IDEAS** Think of three times in your life when you were in a frightening or dangerous situation. Make some brief notes.

Critical Thinking **Tip**

Activity B asks you to **organize** your ideas in a chart. **Organizing** your ideas before you speak makes your ideas easier for listeners to understand.

B. **ORGANIZE IDEAS** Choose one event from Activity A to tell a story about. Then complete the chart.

When and where did it happen?	Who was there?	What happened?
How did you feel?	**What did you do?**	**How did the story end?**

C. **SPEAK** Work in a group. Take turns telling your stories. Use your notes from the chart in Activity B to help you. Refer to the Self-Assessment checklist below before you begin.

iQ **ONLINE** Go online for your alternate Unit Assignment.

CHECK AND REFLECT

A. **CHECK** Think about the Unit Assignment as you complete the Self-Assessment checklist.

SELF-ASSESSMENT		
Yes	No	
☐	☐	I was able to speak easily about the topic.
☐	☐	My partner/group/class understood me.
☐	☐	I used *so* and *such* with adjectives.
☐	☐	I used vocabulary from the unit.
☐	☐	I expressed emotions, such as surprise, happiness, and sadness.
☐	☐	I linked vowel sounds with /w/ or /y/ correctly.

iQ ONLINE **B.** **REFLECT** Go to the Online Discussion Board to discuss these questions.

1. What is something new you learned in this unit?

2. Look back at the Unit Question—When is it good to be afraid? Is your answer different now than when you started the unit? If yes, how is it different? Why?

TRACK YOUR SUCCESS

Circle the words, phrases, and expressions you have learned in this unit.

Nouns	**Adjectives**	You can say that again.
anxiety	ideal	Are you serious?
ground 🔑	negative 🔑 AWL	No kidding!
nightmare	normal 🔑 AWL	No way!
phobia	terrified	I'm glad to hear that.
purpose 🔑		That's wonderful.
strength 🔑	**Phrasal Verbs**	Super.
	get over	How awful.
Verbs	get used to	I'm sorry to hear that.
bother 🔑		That's terrible!
panic	**Idioms and Expressions**	
sweat 🔑	Have a seat.	
	I'm all ears.	
	shaking like a leaf	

🔑 Oxford 2000 keywords
AWL Academic Word List

Check (✓) the skills you learned. If you need more work on a skill, refer to the page(s) in parentheses.

NOTE TAKING	☐ I can use the Cornell method when taking notes. (p. 169)
LISTENING	☐ I can listen for examples. (p. 175)
VOCABULARY	☐ I can recognize and use idioms and expressions. (p. 179)
GRAMMAR	☐ I can recognize and use *so* and *such* with adjectives. (p. 181)
PRONUNCIATION	☐ I can link vowel sounds with /w/ or /y/. (p. 182)
SPEAKING	☐ I can express emotion. (p. 183)
UNIT OBJECTIVE ▶▶▶▶	☐ I can gather information and ideas to describe a frightening experience.

AUTHORS AND CONSULTANTS

Author

Jaimie Scanlon is a freelance ELT materials writer/editor and teacher trainer. She holds a Master's degree in TESOL and French from the School for International Training, where she concentrated on language pedagogy, applied linguistics, and curriculum design. Over the past 20 years, she has taught English language learners of all ages and has trained teachers in Asia, Eastern Europe, and the U.S. She lives in southern Vermont with her husband and two children.

Series Consultants

ONLINE INTEGRATION

Chantal Hemmi holds an Ed.D. TEFL and is a Japan-based teacher trainer and curriculum designer. Since leaving her position as Academic Director of the British Council in Tokyo, she has been teaching at the Center for Language Education and Research at Sophia University on an EAP/CLIL program offered for undergraduates. She delivers lectures and teacher trainings throughout Japan, Indonesia, and Malaysia.

COMMUNICATIVE GRAMMAR

Nancy Schoenfeld holds an M.A. in TESOL from Biola University in La Mirada, California, and has been an English language instructor since 2000. She has taught ESL in California and Hawaii, and EFL in Thailand and Kuwait. She has also trained teachers in the United States and Indonesia. Her interests include teaching vocabulary, extensive reading, and student motivation. She is currently an English Language Instructor at Kuwait University.

WRITING

Marguerite Ann Snow holds a Ph.D. in Applied Linguistics from UCLA. She teaches in the TESOL M.A. program in the Charter College of Education at California State University, Los Angeles. She was a Fulbright scholar in Hong Kong and Cyprus. In 2006, she received the President's Distinguished Professor award at Cal State, LA. She has trained EFL teachers in Algeria, Argentina, Brazil, Egypt, Libya, Morocco, Pakistan, Peru, Spain, and Turkey. She is the author/editor of publications in the areas of integrated content, English for academic purposes, and standards for English teaching and learning. She recently served as a co-editor of *Teaching English as a Second or Foreign Language* (4th ed.).

VOCABULARY

Cheryl Boyd Zimmerman is a Professor at California State University, Fullerton. She specializes in second-language vocabulary acquisition, an area in which she is widely published. She teaches graduate courses on second-language acquisition, culture, vocabulary, and the fundamentals of TESOL and is a frequent invited speaker on topics related to vocabulary teaching and learning. She is the author of *Word Knowledge: A Vocabulary Teacher's Handbook* and Series Director of *Inside Reading*, *Inside Writing*, and *Inside Listening and Speaking*, all published by Oxford University Press.

ASSESSMENT

Lawrence J. Zwier holds an M.A. in TESL from the University of Minnesota. He is currently the Associate Director for Curriculum Development at the English Language Center at Michigan State University in East Lansing. He has taught ESL/EFL in the United States, Saudi Arabia, Malaysia, Japan, and Singapore.

iQ ONLINE extends your learning beyond the classroom. This online content is specifically designed for you! *iQ Online* gives you flexible access to essential content.

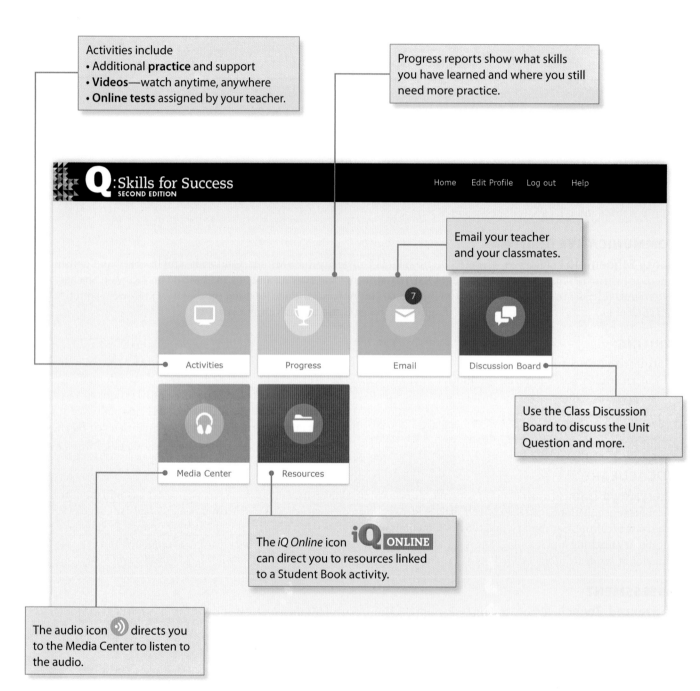

Activities include
• Additional **practice** and support
• **Videos**—watch anytime, anywhere
• **Online tests** assigned by your teacher.

Progress reports show what skills you have learned and where you still need more practice.

Email your teacher and your classmates.

Use the Class Discussion Board to discuss the Unit Question and more.

The *iQ Online* icon **iQ ONLINE** can direct you to resources linked to a Student Book activity.

The audio icon directs you to the Media Center to listen to the audio.

Activities   Progress   Email   Discussion Board

Media Center   Resources

SEE THE INSIDE FRONT COVER FOR HOW TO REGISTER FOR *iQ ONLINE* FOR THE FIRST TIME.

Take Control of Your Learning

You have the choice of where and how you complete the activities. Access your activities and view your progress at any time.

Your teacher may

- assign *iQ Online* as homework,
- do the activities with you in class, or
- let you complete the activities at a pace that is right for you.

iQ Online makes it easy to access everything you need.

Set Clear Goals

STEP 1 If it is your first time, look through the site. See what learning opportunities are available.

STEP 2 The Student Book provides the framework and purpose for each online activity. Before going online, notice the goal of the exercises you are going to do.

STEP 3 Stay on top of your work, following the teacher's instructions.

STEP 4 Use *iQ Online* for review. You can use the materials any time. It is easy for you to do follow-up activities when you have missed a class or want to review.

Manage Your Progress

The activities in *iQ Online* are designed for you to work independently. You can become a confident learner by monitoring your progress and reviewing the activities at your own pace. You may already be used to working online, but if you are not, go to your teacher for guidance.

Check 'View Reports' to monitor your progress. The reports let you track your own progress at a glance. Think about your own performance and set new goals that are right for you, following the teacher's instructions.

iQ Online is a research-based solution specifically designed for English language learners that extends learning beyond the classroom. I hope these steps help you make the most of this essential content.

C. n. Hemm

Chantal Hemmi, EdD TEFL
Center for Language Education and Research
Sophia University, Japan

LISTENING 1 | Places in Danger

UNIT OBJECTIVE ▶▶▶▶ You are going to listen to a report from a travel program. As you listen to the report, gather information and ideas about what the best kind of vacation is.

PREVIEW THE LISTENING

A. VOCABULARY Here are some words from Listening 1. Read their definitions. Then complete each sentence below with the correct word. Change nouns to plural if you need to.

Tip for Success
Pay attention to the listening title. Think about it before you start listening. Ask yourself, *What is this about? What do I know about this topic?*

> **dangerous** (*adjective*) 🎧 may hurt you
> **destroy** (*verb*) 🎧 to break or ruin something
> **insect** (*noun*) 🎧 a small animal with six legs, such as an ant or a fly
> **local** (*adjective*) 🎧 of a place near you
> **pollution** (*noun*) 🎧 dirty air or water
> **shake** (*verb*) 🎧 to move quickly up and down or from side to side
> **tourist** (*noun*) 🎧 a person who visits a place on vacation

🎧 Oxford 2000 keywords

1. If you travel to Mexico, you should try the _____ food. Tacos are my favorite dish.

2. Suddenly, the building started to _____. We all ran outside.

3. Too many visitors could _____ these very old houses.

4. Many big cities have problems with _____. Cars and buses make the air dirty.

5. Many countries need _____ to help the local economy.

6. Do you think it's _____ to travel alone?

7. What kind of _____ is that? It's such a colorful bug.

iQ ONLINE **B.** Go online for more practice with the vocabulary.

54 UNIT 3 | What is the best kind of vacation?

Notice the icon. It directs you to the online materials linked to the Student Book activities.

Q: Skills for Success
SECOND EDITION
Home   Edit Profile   Log out   Help

Mariel Zuarino
My achievements   My grades

1 Sociology
★★★🏆 Excellent! You got 100% of all the points in the unit.

Grammar
average score 76%   completed 23 of 44

2 Nutritional Science
★★★🏆 Well done! You got over 90% of all the points in the unit.

Vocabulary
average score 100%   completed 12 of 72

3 Informational Technology
★★★🏆 You got over 70% of all the points in the unit.

Tests
average score 92%   completed 46 of 62

AUDIO TRACK LIST

Audio can be found in the *iQ Online* Media Center. Go to <u>iQOnlinePractice.com</u>. Click on the Media Center 🎧. Choose to stream or download ⬇ the audio file you select. Not all audio files are available for download.

Page	Track Name: Q2e_01_LS_
2	U01_Q_Classroom.mp3
5	U01_NoteTakingSkill_ActivityA.mp3
7	U01_Listening1_ActivityA.mp3
7	U01_Listening1_ActivityB.mp3
8	U01_Listening1_ActivityF.mp3
9	U01_ListeningSkill_Example.mp3
9	U01_ListeningSkill_ActivityA.mp3
10	U01_ListeningSkill_ActivityB.mp3
11	U01_Listening2_ActivityA.mp3
11	U01_Listening2_ActivityB.mp3
12	U01_Listening2_ActivityC.mp3
19	U01_Pronunciation_Examples.mp3
20	U01_Pronunciation_ActivityB.mp3
21	U01_SpeakingSkill_ActivityA.mp3
21	U01_SpeakingSkill_ActivityB.mp3
27	U02_Q_Classroom.mp3
29	U02_NoteTakingSkill_ActivityA.mp3
31	U02_Listening1_ActivityA.mp3
31	U02_Listening1_ActivityB.mp3
34	U02_ListeningSkill_ActivityA.mp3
34	U02_ListeningSkill_ActivityB.mp3
36	U02_Listening2_ActivityA.mp3
36	U02_Listening2_ActivityC.mp3
40	U02_VocabularySkill_ActivityA.mp3
40	U02_VocabularySkill_ActivityB.mp3
41	U02_Grammar_Part1_ActivityA.mp3
42	U02_Grammar_Part2_ActivityA.mp3
43	U02_Pronunciation_Examples.mp3
44	U02_Pronunciation_ActivityA.mp3
51	U03_Q_Classroom.mp3
53	U03_NoteTakingSkill_Example.mp3
53	U03_NoteTakingSkill_ActivityA.mp3
55	U03_Listening1_ActivityA.mp3
55	U03_Listening1_ActivityC.mp3
56	U03_Listening1_ActivityE.mp3
57	U03_ListeningSkill_Example1.mp3
57	U03_ListeningSkill_Example2.mp3
57	U03_ListeningSkill_Example3.mp3
58	U03_ListeningSkill_ActivityA.mp3
59	U03_ListeningSkill_ActivityC.mp3
61	U03_Listening2_ActivityA.mp3
62	U03_Listening2_ActivityB.mp3
68	U03_Grammar_ActivityB.mp3
69	U03_Pronunciation_Examples.mp3
71	U03_UnitAssignment_ActivityA.mp3
71	U03_UnitAssignment_ActivityB.mp3

Page	Track Name: Q2e_01_LS_
74	U04_Q_Classroom.mp3
78	U04_Listening1_ActivityA.mp3
79	U04_Listening1_ActivityB.mp3
80	U04_ListeningSkill_ActivityA.mp3
81	U04_ListeningSkill_ActivityB.mp3
84	U04_Listening2_ActivityA.mp3
84	U04_Listening2_ActivityB.mp3
89	U04_Grammar_ActivityA.mp3
91	U04_Pronunciation_Examples.mp3
93	U04_SpeakingSkill_Example.mp3
93	U04_SpeakingSkill_ActivityA.mp3
95	U04_UnitAssignment_ActivityB.mp3
95	U04_UnitAssignment_ActivityC.mp3
99	U05_Q_Classroom.mp3
101	U05_NoteTakingSkill_Example.mp3
101	U05_NoteTakingSkill_ActivityA.mp3
103	U05_Listening1_ActivityA.mp3
103	U05_Listening1_ActivityC.mp3
105	U05_ListeningSkill_ActivityA.mp3
107	U05_Listening2_ActivityA.mp3
108	U05_Listening2_ActivityC.mp3
112	U05_Grammar_ActivityA.mp3
114	U05_Pronunciation_Example1.mp3
114	U05_Pronunciation_Example2.mp3
114	U05_Pronunciation_Example3.mp3
115	U05_Pronunciation_ActivityB.mp3
116	U05_UnitAssignment.mp3
120	U06_Q_Classroom.mp3
123	U06_NoteTakingSkill_Example.mp3
123	U06_NoteTakingSkill_ActivityA.mp3
125	U06_Listening1_ActivityA.mp3
126	U06_Listening1_ActivityC.mp3
128	U06_ListeningSkill_ActivityA.mp3
128	U06_ListeningSkill_ActivityB.mp3
130	U06_Listening2_ActivityA.mp3
131	U06_Listening2_ActivityE.mp3
133	U06_VocabularySkill_ActivityA.mp3
136	U06_Pronunciation_Examples.mp3
137	U06_Pronunciation_ActivityA.mp3
138	U06_SpeakingSkill_ActivityA.mp3
139	U06_UnitAssignment.mp3

Page	Track Name: Q2e_01_LS_
142	U07_Q_Classroom.mp3
147	U07_Listening1_ActivityA.mp3
147	U07_Listening1_ActivityC.mp3
149	U07_ListeningSkill_ActivityA.mp3
152	U07_Listening2_ActivityA.mp3
152	U07_Listening2_ActivityB.mp3
155	U07_VocabularySkill_ActivityA.mp3
159	U07_Pronunciation_Examples.mp3
159	U07_Pronunciation_ActivityA.mp3
159	U07_Pronunciation_ActivityB.mp3
160	U07_NoteTakingSkill_Example.mp3
161	U07_NoteTakingSkill_ActivityA.mp3
162	U07_UnitAssignment.mp3
167	U08_Q_Classroom.mp3
172	U08_Listening1_ActivityA.mp3
173	U08_Listening1_ActivityB.mp3
175	U08_ListeningSkill_ActivityA.mp3
177	U08_Listening2_ActivityA.mp3
177	U08_Listening2_ActivityB.mp3
182	U08_Pronunciation_Example1.mp3
182	U08_Pronunciation_Example2.mp3
183	U08_Pronunciation_ActivityB.mp3
185	U08_UnitAssignment.mp3

🔑 The keywords of the **Oxford 2000** have been carefully selected by a group of language experts and experienced teachers as the words which should receive priority in vocabulary study because of their importance and usefulness.

AWL The Academic Word List is the most principled and widely accepted list of academic words. Averil Coxhead gathered information from academic materials across the academic disciplines to create this word list.

The Common European Framework of Reference for Languages (CEFR) provides a basic description of what language learners have to do to use language effectively. The system contains 6 reference levels: **A1, A2, B1, B2, C1, C2**. CEFR leveling provided by the Word Family Framework, created by Richard West and published by the British Council. http://www.learnenglish.org.uk/wff/

UNIT 1

advertising *(n.)*, **B1**
application *(n.)*, **A2**
assistant *(n.)* **AWL**, **B1**
basic *(adj.)* 🔑, **A1**
career *(n.)* 🔑, **A1**
degree *(n.)* 🔑, **B1**
employee *(n.)*, **B1**
graduate *(v.)*, **B1**
interview *(n.)* 🔑, **A2**
major *(n.)* **AWL**, **B2**
manager *(n.)* 🔑, **A1**
organized *(adj.)* 🔑, **B2**
requirement *(n.)* **AWL**, **A2**
résumé *(n.)*, **B1**

UNIT 2

avoid *(v.)* 🔑, **A1**
bottom *(n.)* 🔑, **A2**
carefully *(adv.)* 🔑, **A2**
confused *(adj.)* 🔑, **B1**
custom *(n.)* 🔑, **A2**
death *(n.)* 🔑, **A1**
die *(v.)* 🔑, **A1**
difficulty *(n.)* 🔑, **A2**
international *(adj.)* 🔑, **A1**
invite *(v.)* 🔑, **A2**
mistake *(n.)* 🔑, **A2**

offended *(adj.)*, **B1**
positive *(adj.)* 🔑 **AWL**, **A1**
rude *(adj.)* 🔑, **B1**
upset *(adj.)* 🔑, **A2**
wedding *(n.)* 🔑, **A2**

UNIT 3

ancient *(adj.)* 🔑, **A2**
dangerous *(adj.)* 🔑, **A2**
destroy *(v.)* 🔑, **A2**
enjoyable *(adj.)* 🔑, **B1**
insect *(n.)* 🔑, **A2**
lead *(v.)* 🔑, **A1**
local *(adj.)* 🔑, **A1**
pollution *(n.)* 🔑, **B1**
population *(n.)*, **A1**
prepare *(v.)* 🔑, **A1**
pretty *(adj.)* 🔑, **B1**
repair *(v.)* 🔑, **A2**
shake *(v.)* 🔑, **A2**
tourist *(n.)* 🔑, **B1**
volunteer *(n.)* **AWL**, **B1**

UNIT 4

afraid *(adj.)* 🔑, **A1**
comical *(adj.)*, **B2**
communicate *(v.)* 🔑 **AWL**, **B1**
describe *(v.)* 🔑, **A1**
feelings *(n.)* 🔑, **A2**

hit *(n.)* 🔑, **B1**
however *(adv.)* 🔑, **A2**
huge *(adj.)* 🔑, **A1**
imagine *(v.)* 🔑, **A2**
make fun of *(phr. v.)*, **B2**
probably *(adv.)* 🔑, **A2**
professional *(adj.)* 🔑 **AWL**, **A1**
sense of humor *(phr.)*, **B1**
talented *(adj.)*, **B1**
understand *(v.)* 🔑, **A1**
wrong *(adj.)* 🔑, **A1**

UNIT 5

active *(adj.)* 🔑, **A1**
benefit *(n.)* 🔑 **AWL**, **A1**
brain *(n.)* 🔑, **A2**
coach *(n.)*, **B1**
concentrate *(v.)* 🔑 **AWL**, **A2**
escape *(v.)* 🔑, **A2**
exciting *(adj.)* 🔑, **B1**
forget *(v.)* 🔑, **A1**
human *(n.)* 🔑, **A2**
improve *(v.)* 🔑, **A2**
lower stress *(phr. v.)*, **B1**
patient *(adj.)* 🔑, **B1**
protect *(v.)* 🔑, **A1**
skill *(n.)* 🔑, **A1**
traditional *(adj.)* **AWL**, **A1**

UNIT 6

according to *(phr.)* 🔑, A1
cheat *(v.)* 🔑, B1
get caught *(phr.)*, B1
grade *(n.)* 🔑 AWL, B1
illegal *(adj.)* 🔑 AWL, A2
lie *(n.)* 🔑, B1
a little bit *(phr.)*, A1
quarter *(n.)* 🔑, A2
responsibility *(n.)* 🔑, B1
section *(n.)* 🔑 AWL, A1
so far *(phr.)*, B1
suffer *(v.)* 🔑, A1
survey *(n.)* AWL, A1
technology *(n.)* 🔑 AWL, A1

UNIT 7

accept *(v.)* 🔑, A1
achieve *(v.)* 🔑 AWL, A1
advice *(n.)* 🔑, A2
change your mind *(phr. v.)*, B1
encourage *(v.)* 🔑, A1
especially *(adv.)* 🔑, A1
flexible *(adj.)* AWL, B1
goal *(n.)* 🔑 AWL, A2
habit *(n.)* 🔑, B1
opportunity *(n.)* 🔑, A1
progress *(n.)* 🔑, A2
proverb *(n.)*, C1
recommend *(v.)* 🔑, A2
remain *(v.)* 🔑, A1
remind *(v.)* 🔑, A2
stick to *(phr. v.)*, B2

UNIT 8

anxiety *(n.)*, B1
bother *(v.)*, 🔑, B1
get over *(phr. v.)*, B1
get used to *(phr. v.)*, A2
ground *(n.)* 🔑, A1
ideal *(adj.)*, B1
negative *(adj.)* 🔑 AWL, A2
nightmare *(n.)*, B2
normal *(adj.)* 🔑 AWL, A1
panic *(v.)*, B2
phobia *(n.)*, B2
purpose *(n.)* 🔑, A1
strength *(n.)* 🔑, A1
sweat *(v.)* 🔑, B2
terrified *(adj.)*, B1